Praise for *The Ultimate RPG Gameplay Guide*

"James D'Amato is one of those rare st
those delightful and unexpected cho
their eyes go wide, but he has that second, rarer gift. When doing it, he
can build upon what's already been established, weaving a little more
and passing the tapestry to someone else to be inspired from."

—Alan Linic, writer for *Saturday Night Live*
and cohost of the *tl;dm* podcast

"Look, I'm gonna level with you: James D'Amato is doing the coolest,
most exciting, and original work in tabletop game design right now
and provides a truly vast assortment of tools and techniques for you
to immediately and profoundly improve the narrative experience of
your game. If I were you, I'd be getting this book in my hands as fast
as possible!"

—Brennan Lee Mulligan, host of *CollegeHumor*'s
Dimension 20 D&D RPG show

"I've been role-playing for thirty-five years and I'm still learning how
to make our sessions more fun and more emotionally resonant by
listening to the great *One Shot* podcast. James has put together a
great collection of ideas that'll appeal to a wide range of players, from
newbies to old hands."

—John Rogers, writer and showrunner for *Leverage*,
The Librarians, and *Jackie Chan Adventures*

THE ULTIMATE
RPG
GAMEPLAY
GUIDE

THE ULTIMATE

RPG

GAMEPLAY GUIDE

ROLE-PLAY THE BEST CAMPAIGN EVER— NO MATTER THE GAME!

INCLUDES INSTRUCTIONS, PROMPTS, ACTIVITIES, AND MORE

JAMES D'AMATO

ADAMS MEDIA

NEW YORK   LONDON   TORONTO   SYDNEY   NEW DELHI

Adams Media
An Imprint of Simon & Schuster, Inc.
100 Technology Center Drive
Stoughton, MA 02072

First Adams Media trade paperback edition October 2019

ADAMS MEDIA and colophon are trademarks of Simon & Schuster.

For information about special discounts for bulk purchases, please contact Simon & Schuster Special Sales at 1-866-506-1949 or business@simonandschuster.com.

The Simon & Schuster Speakers Bureau can bring authors to your live event. For more information or to book an event contact the Simon & Schuster Speakers Bureau at 1-866-248-3049 or visit our website at www.simonspeakers.com.

Interior design by Colleen Cunningham
Dice image © 123RF/sudowoodo

Manufactured in China

10 9 8 7

Library of Congress Cataloging-in-Publication Data
Names: D'Amato, James, author.
Title: The ultimate RPG gameplay guide / James D'Amato.
Description: Avon, Massachusetts: Adams Media, 2019.
Series: The ultimate RPG guide series.
Includes bibliographical references and index.
Identifiers: LCCN 2019023190 | ISBN 9781507210932 (pb) | ISBN 9781507210949 (ebook)
Subjects: LCSH: Fantasy games. | Role playing. | Internet games.
Classification: LCC GV1469.6 .D36 2019 | DDC 793.93--dc23
LC record available at https://lccn.loc.gov/2019023190

ISBN 978-1-5072-1093-2
ISBN 978-1-5072-1094-9 (ebook)

To my parents Cathy and Cliff, who made sure
I learned all the skills I needed to write a book,
and to my spouse, Mel, who supported me while
I attempted the impossible a second time.

Contents

Introduction...12

Defining Terms...13

PART 1

BASIC STORYTELLING   17

1   Understanding Audience...19
An introduction to thinking of the players of an RPG as the audience for the story.

2   Stating Objective...28
An explanation of how creating clear goals aids collaboration.

3   Story- or System-Led Creation...36
An explanation of how game mechanics are used to create narrative.

4   Session Zero...45
A guide for having a conversation before you start playing a formal game to help your group work together.

5   Understanding Text...58
An explanation of how specific words shape a group's understanding of the narrative and ability to collaborate.

6   Make Choices Important...69
An explanation of concepts from improv and how they apply to games.

7   Pacing...87
Multifaceted advice on what drives the audience experience of an RPG story and how to pace it effectively.

8   Engagement...100
Explanation of vulnerability and enthusiasm as a driving force in narrative games. Alternative methods for encouraging those core drivers.

PART 2

ADVANCED PLAYING TECHNIQUES   107

9   Introduction to GMing Style and
Making Choices with Intention...109
An explanation of different stylistic approaches to GMing and
advice on how to cultivate a personal style.

10   Themes...120
A guide to understanding themes in RPG stories and how to
use them to create a cohesive piece.

11   Imagery...135
An explanation of how to use themes to create imagery in your
narration.

12   Playing to Change...149
An explanation of how PCs are different from protagonists in
other media and advice to help you play characters who feel
dynamic.

13   Looking for Trouble...162
Advice for eschewing traditional approaches to playing a PC in
order to introduce compelling conflict to a story.

14   Delegating Creativity...173
Advice to allow GMs to delegate parts of their role to make a
game more collaborative and engaging.

PART 3

PLAYING FOR EXPERIENCE   185

15   Finding a Voice...187
A drill exercise for generating and practicing character voices.

16   Limiting Choices...190
A storytelling exercise challenging players to creatively
overcome obstacles while limiting their choices.

17   Same Rock, Different World...193
An exercise using shifting genre and theme to change
descriptions of objects in different settings.

18   Building the Group Mind...200
Three exercises adapted from improv to develop collaborative
skills in an RPG group.

19   Unpacking Desire...205
A self-analytical tool to aid players in understanding which
aspects of RPGs they enjoy.

20   Narrative Rewards Table...211
A tool to help GMs generate story hooks as rewards for quests
rather than loot.

21   Pacing Scorecard...213
Tools to help GMs outline sessions by breaking down different
factors that affect a game's pace.

22   Mood Lighting...220
Similar to Same Rock, this exercise guides readers to use the
same details to make a room appropriate for different moods,
tones, and scene types.

23   Side Scenes...227
Three exercises based on improv and fan fiction to help players
explore their characters outside regular game sessions.

Glossary...**235**

Acknowledgments and Additional Resources...**241**

Index...**243**

Introduction

Maybe you're just hearing about role-playing games. Or maybe you used to play a long time ago, but you haven't picked up your bag of polyhedral dice in years. Or maybe you're playing in a game right now, but you feel as if you want to get more out of it.

Whatever the case, there's no doubt that RPGs have been getting a lot of attention lately. Millions of people around the world play them every week. They've been featured in TV shows and on blogs and podcasts. On the surface, they seem pretty simple: a bunch of people sitting around a **table**, telling a story, and rolling dice and checking charts to see what the player characters should do next. But there's a lot more that goes into your gameplay than just statistics and rolling dice. That's because each of the players has created a character, and that character is *taking part* in the story. The story might be about anything—your character could be exploring dungeons in search of treasure or piloting a starship to the farthest reaches of the galaxy. The only limit is the imaginations of you and your fellow gamers.

If you're running a player character, you want to get the most out of their actions—from finding your character's voice and motivation to understanding the overall pace of action in the game. If you're a game master, you set the theme for the game, and you want to make sure the players are having fun while also finding the world they're in compelling and exciting. This book is full of advice and exercises to help you get the most from your gaming experience.

Role-playing games are about shared storytelling, so in the first part you'll explore that specifically—how to tell and interact with a story that draws you into itself. In the second part of the book, you'll look at how to make your game world richer and deeper through voice, imagery, and themes. Finally, in the third part you'll find some fun exercises to make your gameplay more imaginative and, well, fun. Because the world of role-playing games is all about having fun.

So get started! There are a lot of worlds out there to explore!

Defining Terms

B efore we tackle the issue of how to make your role-playing game experience richer, deeper, and more enjoyable, we need to get our basic terminology right. If you've played RPGs before, this will seem pretty elementary, but if you're new to this world, this section will make clear a lot that may be confusing to you. For clarity's sake, important words and terms will appear in bold type throughout this book.

What Is an RPG?

A **role-playing game (RPG)** is a type of game where players generate stories through shared imagination. The core concept behind RPGs is similar to imagination games you might have played when you were young. Remember playing "house," using dolls or action figures, and other simple games of pretend? These all call on players to inhabit a role and interact in a shared imaginary space.

Tabletop RPGs published in game manuals introduce structure to this process. Published RPGs, or **role-playing systems**, help players establish goals, track abstract information, and resolve conflicts. Rule systems and **randomizers** (usually dice) help adults make sense of what comes naturally to most children.

The first and most famous example of a published RPG is *Dungeons & Dragons*, first published in 1974. It defined what most people picture when they think of RPGs. This sword and sorcery fantasy with polyhedral dice is still immensely popular. However, RPGs have grown well beyond these roots to encompass every genre imaginable.

Folks benefit from RPGs in a number of ways beyond simple entertainment. RPGs foster communication skills, empathy, and creative problem-solving ability, and they provide a fantastic outlet for creative expression. For some players, creative expression is the most appealing aspect of play. Stories built with RPGs have become their own form of entertainment called **actual play**, where groups record or stream their game **sessions** for an audience.

If you discovered RPGs though actual play productions like *One Shot*, *Critical Role*, or *The Adventure Zone* this book will help break down some of the storytelling techniques you've seen and help you develop those skills. If you're new to RPGs in general, this book will help you avoid common problems people encounter when first trying to collaborate to create stories. If you're an experienced player with your own style, this book can help you break down what you like about the way you play. Maybe it will even help you discover a new reason to love these games.

No matter what brought you here, we can all agree you did a stellar job in purchasing or receiving this book as a gift. Turns out, it's exactly what you needed.

Before we dive in there are a few roles you should understand.

PCs and GMs

Everyone involved in an RPG is playing the game and is therefore a **player**. When we refer to players in this book, we mean everyone at the table. Traditional RPGs have specific roles that work differently to make the game function. Broadly speaking the most popular meta roles are **player character (PC)** and **game master (GM)**.

WHAT IS A PC?

In most games, the majority of people participating are responsible for controlling individual characters. For our purposes these characters and the people who play them are PCs.

Narratively, PCs are the protagonists, and players in the PC role are the primary authors of their story. PC players choose how their character thinks, looks, and acts. PCs interact with outside forces like other players and randomization; so a player in a PC role can't control everything that happens to their character. However, a PC player always controls how their character reacts.

Players in the PC role can have the following responsibilities:

● Determining their character's appearance, behavior, personality, and history

- Making decisions about their character's actions
- Embodying their character's voice
- Managing their character's statistics and abilities
- Addressing storytelling challenges through character action

These responsibilities and the overall function of this role can vary from game to game. In some games, the most important aspects of a PC are numbers that make up their vital statistics. Others call for players to pay attention to their character's emotional state based on events in the game. And some games focus on both.

WHAT IS A GM?

Many RPGs have a specialized role that controls any elements of the game that are not PC. The title for this role varies, but here we'll refer to it as the game master (GM).

The GM is like a narrator, director, producer, supporting actor, and crew rolled into one person. Colloquially we say the GM "**runs**" the game. The GM is usually also the arbiter of a game's rules. Sometimes there are no clear rules in a game system for what's happening; sometimes there are a few contradictory rules that might apply. The GM is tasked with deciding what to do in those situations. The GM is also role-playing. They control the actions of **non-player characters** (NPCs), which function to support or oppose PCs in the story.

Players in the GM role can have the following responsibilities:

- Determining the appearance, behavior, and personality of NPCs
- Controlling forces in the game world unrelated to characters, such as environment and time
- Controlling the general flow and focus of the overall narrative
- Presenting PCs with challenges that advance their story
- Preparing materials for game sessions
- Understanding the rules of the game and deciding when they apply

FRIEND NOT FOE

Some people interpret the GM role as adversarial to the players, as the GM controls all of the challenges that impede or threaten the PCs. The decision to view the GM as a kind of adversary is ultimately up to the GM and players, but we generally advise against it because it can create social tensions that make it difficult to have fun.

The number and variety of responsibilities a player in the GM role has varies based on game system and personal style.

GMs AND SOCIAL DYNAMICS

GMs often have a position of authority at the table. Even if this authority is just in the realm of the game, it affects the social dynamics of the play group. It can create a perceived power imbalance between players. Recognizing these dynamics will help you avoid some of the conflicts that surround games.

Now that we've established who does what in a game, let's talk about the way we construct the stories within the game.

PART 1

Basic Storytelling

You're probably familiar with a lot of the ideas we're going to cover in this section based on literature classes you took in school. If you've also had experience in creative writing or film criticism you'll see familiar ideas. Academic resources are tools and we can use them how we like. An axe is intended for labor, but swinging one at zombies makes it fun! (That was terrible! Please send all complaints about bad jokes to fakeemailaddress@forthebit.com.)

In Part 1 we'll reframe a lot of conventional storytelling wisdom through the lens of RPGs. We'll also break down some very basic ideas that experienced role players probably understand intuitively. Taking the time to review the fundamentals this way will help you develop good storytelling techniques down the road.

With that out of the way, let's get rolling!

Understanding Audience

In this chapter, we'll explore how the structure of RPGs sets them apart from other storytelling mediums. Then we'll discuss how that structure should frame your choices during play.

What Does *Audience* Mean to a Story?

Audience actively shapes the creative process. One of the basic questions creators ask themselves when starting a project is, Who is this for? The kinds of stories you tell and the way you tell them varies widely based on who you think will listen.

Not everyone actively creates for an audience, but we still make choices surrounding audience all the time. For example, you wouldn't show a friend who hates horror movies your favorite slasher film. Even if you love it, you know your friend won't appreciate what makes it great. Being mindful of your friend's tastes ensures you'll both have a better time.

Story and audience shape one another. This is one of the things that makes RPGs so interesting.

How Are RPGs Different?

In RPGs the audience is also creating the story by interacting with each other. You and your fellow players are enjoying your game's story as you are writing it. The process of creating that story is as important to the success of a game as the story itself.

Books and movies are assessed as complete works. In games, moment-to-moment engagement far outweighs values such as plot momentum that are critical to other mediums. It's possible for a two-hour shopping sequence—which has nothing to do with the plot—to be more relevant to the overall fun of a game than a dramatic character reveal.

This unusual audience perspective means a lot of conventional storytelling advice doesn't apply to stories told through RPGs. In the play *Hamlet*, for example, a large number of characters die to advance the central character's story. While in an RPG you can certainly kill a character to advance the plot, killing a PC will cut someone out of the game. You don't want to kill the king of Denmark at the start of a game if it means one player is going to spend most of their time with nothing to do. Even if the resulting story is as riveting as *Hamlet*.

Different aspects of storytelling are important based on how the narrative is being presented. For example, if we were to tell the story of Cinderella out loud, we only need to say the dress her fairy godmother gives her is "beautiful." An audience listening can fill in the details as they like. Their details won't impact your telling of the story. If we were instead preparing to film an adaptation of Cinderella, the details of her dress become important. The audience is going to see a dress, and you have to make them see it as beautiful.

The **medium** changes how an audience engages with the story. In a movie, a dress has to visually provoke a specific reaction. When the story is being told verbally, the audience needs to get enough information to form their own imaginary vision of a beautiful dress.

In RPGs a player—the audience—is expected to inhabit the role of Cinderella. That makes entirely different information relevant. Does the dress affect her abilities beyond making her look like she belongs at a fancy ball? Does she have to accept the dress or can she request a suit? Will the dress be able to conceal a dagger she can use to slay the stepmother and avenge her father's murder? We may even need to know if the dress has its own hit points!

Even when you are a GM, you are still a member of the audience. The world and story you manage for the PCs still needs to entertain you. Otherwise it won't be fun to play.

WHERE'S THE PARTY?

To better understand the audience structure of games, let's look at your favorite stories as if they were games.

✏ First write down your favorite stories from books, movies, or TV:

✏ Now answer the following questions:

Who are the PCs in this story?

Could this potentially fit 4–6 players?

Would a group of players have fun following the story as it is written or told?

How might the story change if a player needed more for their character to do?

Being aware of who the audience is will help you more consistently play to the tastes of your group. It will also empower you to take stock of your own desires and orient them toward a narratively fulfilling experience.

RAILROAD CROSSING

One of the most common complaints about GM technique is something called railroading. Essentially this means that the GM isn't allowing players to make meaningful choices that deviate from a predetermined critical path. In other words, players are being restricted to observing a larger story that moves without them—they're on a narrative "railroad."

Often the storytelling instincts behind railroading are good. If you were to script the gaming session as a novel, you could arrange the characters as you like and tell a great story. However, in games the ability for players to drive the story is more important than the overall story structure.

There are lots of GM behaviors that can create a feeling of railroad play. This book will help you identify and avoid those behaviors.

Getting to Know Yourself

The audience member you have the deepest connection to is yourself! When playing an RPG, one of your primary duties is to make sure that you are having fun. Everyone at the table is there to help you, but you have the greatest insight into what makes you tick. Whether you are a PC or a GM you have to make sure that the game brings you some kind of fulfillment.

Unraveling the mystery of how we operate as audience members can be tricky. For some of us, pleasing ourselves is a feat we can only accomplish some of the time. Plenty of people are comfortable saying whether or not they enjoyed a story, but it can be difficult to understand why, let alone to know what needs to change to make the story a better one.

It's impossible to ensure that you'll be satisfied by a game 100 percent of the time, even if you're working really hard at it. What you can do is be analytical about your experiences to help yourself make choices that will set you up for success.

TOTAL EXPERIENCE

Some folks choose to watch movies they think are bad, just for fun. For them, the process of mocking or deconstructing something truly awful is part of a larger enjoyable experience. In learning to understand which aspects of RPGs you like, you'll need to understand the components that make up your overall experience. Knowing yourself is being able to say "I like making fun of bad movies" rather than "I have fun watching bad movies."

Chapter 19 of this book will help you break down what you like to do in RPGs and give you a general idea of what you want to pursue when you're at the table. Your enjoyment is shaped primarily by a few important big decisions you make when preparing to play, and countless small decisions you make throughout the game.

The role-playing system you choose, the role of GM or PC, and even individual character abilities will affect how you engage with the game. Playing a mechanically robust game could place a lot of importance on learning and understanding rules. Playing a canny negotiator might mean a lot of speaking in character. GMing a sci-fi game could mean describing lots of horrific alien monsters. A few top-level choices will greatly influence what you do in a game. That will have a dramatic effect on your experience.

Once your game starts, you'll be faced with countless situations where you'll have to choose how to engage with a given scene. Playing with a narrative approach will sometimes call on you to make choices that challenge your desires. A strong thuggish brute is well suited to solving problems with their fists, and that might be what you enjoy most. However, occasionally watching your character sweat through a delicate social situation can make that next fistfight all the more satisfying.

Of course, RPGs are more than personal choices. You're at the table with a whole group of people, and your experience will be at least partially dictated by what other people want to do. When you're watching out for yourself as an audience member, your job isn't to make sure every scene is geared toward your tastes; it's to ensure there is space for what you like in the overall experience. Otherwise your games become work.

Playing to Expectations

The other players at the table are also part of the audience. You can't realistically expect to keep track of everyone's personal preferences. However, if you're aware of some key structural audience expectations, you can make it easy for people to find their own fun.

Complaints about player behavior are usually prompted by mismatched expectations. Let's take a look at a few common expectations to be aware of in different roles.

GMs: PROBLEMS MAKE OPPORTUNITIES

Engaging the audience as a GM partially means helping PCs find something for their characters to do. A big part of GMing is looking for diverse challenges that will allow everyone in the group to contribute to the game. When we discuss pacing in Chapter 7, you'll get a better idea of why you want to vary scene types. For now, it's important to remember that part of your motivation should be the desire to create opportunities that play to the strengths of individual PCs.

The role of a protagonist in a narrative is generally to be a problem solver. It's easier for PCs to pull themselves into the action if you put them in challenging situations they think they can solve. A hotshot getaway driver doesn't have much to do if there are no high-speed chases.

PCs: ONE FOR ALL

PCs are capable of anything. That doesn't mean they are likely to overcome every challenge successfully. It means anything they do—whether successful or unsuccessful—has the potential to drive the plot forward. As a PC, you can influence the experience of other players based on how you decide to apply your involvement with the story.

The challenges that drive stories in **traditional** RPGs are meant to be addressed by a team of characters with varied strengths and weaknesses. PCs who play to their own strengths aren't guaranteed success, but they give the group the best chance of succeeding. Ideally, when you make a move as a PC you want to play in your portion of the spotlight, not steal it from someone else.

No one chooses a bad roll. Sometimes players choose to take the spotlight when their character isn't suited for the task at hand, with unfortunate results. It's especially frustrating to suffer the consequences of a failed action if there was another PC better suited for that moment.

The same holds true for self-destructive choices. It's cool to punch the chief of police if everyone wants to have their character's job on the line. It's not fun if one player is exploring a personal plot that gets in the way of the party's goals. Choices built around an awareness of the group as a whole are more likely to please the players.

GMs: FOCUS ON THE PARTY

It's easy to get caught up chasing the narrative of the world, especially when PC choices provoke interesting consequences. However, the majority of the audience only has agency over the story when it revolves around PCs. Devoting too much focus to a world outside the PCs runs the risk of alienating the audience.

It's really cool if the PC's latest job caused chaos for the city's criminal underworld. Following a new gang moving in on recently vacated territory is only interesting if the PCs actively discover that information. Interrogating a new mafia foot soldier is exciting. Watching two NPCs discuss mob politics without the party isn't.

Anytime the PCs are watching events unfold without the chance to be meaningfully involved, they're sitting on a railroad. Part of creating agency for players is orienting the audience perspective around events that directly involve the PCs.

PCs: SEPARATING AUDIENCE AND CHARACTER

Certain fictional archetypes present a real challenge to RPG audiences. Thieves who steal from their friends and badass loners who refuse to cooperate are fun in most stories but suffer in RPGs. In most media these archetypes create compelling tension between characters, which is fun. In RPGs they create tension between the character and *the audience*, which is distinctly *not* fun.

You *can* tell interesting RPG stories with archetypes that call for acting against the group, but they need to be grounded in creating opportunities for other players. A pickpocket taking gold from a fellow PC limits that player's access to resources. It's disruptive and hurtful. A pickpocket taking a diary and discovering the fighter is a princess in disguise opens up new opportunities to engage in that character's backstory.

Actual Play

Narrative advice for RPGs starts to look more conventional when a game is used to create **actual play (AP)**. AP games are recorded or streamed for a nonparticipating audience to enjoy. The viewing audience won't necessarily have an impact on your game because they aren't playing, but their presence will affect how you play.

In unrecorded games the decisions you make affect yourself and the other players at the table. Actual play expands your audience and the number of people affected by your choices. At a table, you can actively check in with your friends. With an unseen audience, you don't have the same ability to communicate, which makes it easier to take an action that upsets people. The content of traditional games is ephemeral—it lives and dies in memory. Recording means your words stick around longer. Players in AP have far greater accountability than players in a regular game. Not everyone is suited to that kind of performance-centered environment.

AP also shifts the focus of audience enjoyment away from the players' own experiences. A good deal of the action in RPGs is internal—meaning part of the story exists in a place an external audience can't appreciate. Having outside observers can mean implicit moments have to become explicit. A conversation between two PCs full of veiled references to a shared past can be really satisfying for the people involved, but it could leave an external audience feeling out of the loop. In this instance AP demands players fold exposition of their character concepts into the narrative, or find another way to frame the events of their story. It's all part of the small changes that need to happen when your audience dynamic shifts.

Finally, there is a contrast between observing audiences and participating audiences in how they experience rewards. Awarding PCs with wealth and **experience (XP)** opens characters up to new opportunities. Part of the fun is players imagining new possibilities for themselves as those experience points move them up through the levels of the game. It doesn't have the same impact for people who don't directly control the story. An observing audience might still enjoy seeing a hero receive a reward, but it won't hold the same significance. The levels of satisfaction are totally different.

AP games are still games, but the structure of an external audience can alter a group's approach and priorities. When developing an RPG for AP, it's important to consider how that structure might affect your fun.

Stating Objective

Problems at RPG tables are usually rooted in miscommunication, and most of that is caused by mismatched expectations. Players can avoid these problems by establishing a set of common **objectives** for their game. Objectives are goals for the story, characters, and tone of the game. Bringing them into the open helps ensure everyone is after the same thing.

Imagine a film where half the cast is looking to create a heady award-winning film and the other half wants to make a lighthearted action blockbuster. Both approaches to filmmaking have their own conventions. What works for one won't necessarily work for the other. Even if everyone in the cast is doing their best, they will have serious problems accomplishing either goal. The same concept is true for RPGs. When you haven't talked about what everybody wants, players have the potential to get in each other's way.

In this chapter, we're going to look at which choices are influenced by a group's objective and why that's important to the story.

Picking a Game

RPGs are a diverse medium, and there are thousands of different games. To a certain extent, you can tell any story with any game system. You *can* play emotional stories using a system primarily concerned with how many cool guns you can fit on a big robot. However, it's worth taking note of when a game supports what you want and when it gets in your way.

Ultimately RPGs are tool kits that players can engage and ignore as they like. There are plenty of possibilities a group might encounter that won't fit into the structure a designer foresaw when writing the manual. Game designers work to craft systems with specific goals and audiences in mind. If you don't think rolling handfuls of dice, spending action points, or pulling bricks from a jumbling tower is fun, it's probably not the best idea to commit to a game that asks you to do any of those things often.

Here's an example that will help illustrate this point. Rebecca and Sanjay want to play a game about two tough-as-nails orc mercenaries who hate and love each other in equal measure. They're caught between two games because they can see their story fitting into either system:

GLOOMSPRINTER	CROSSED STARS
Genre: Fantasy Cyberpunk	**Genre: Romance**
An urban fantasy cyberpunk RPG about mercenaries living on the edge of the law in a dystopian future. This game features robust options for combat. It has a dozen fighting skills applicable in various situations. Granular factors like terrain, weather, and a character's physical health can influence each action. Most scenes revolve around rolling fistfuls of dice.	A game that can be applied to many potential settings where the romantic tension is represented by a wooden jumbling tower. If the tower falls, someone acts on feelings they are trying to repress. The game revolves around scenes that increase intimacy between characters, slowly making the tower more unstable. Anything can happen in a game of *Crossed Stars*, but the only action it mechanically supports is intimate tension.

Gloomsprinter has lots of options for playing mercenaries, and *Crossed Stars* absolutely supports romance.

If both players are interested in the moment-to-moment choices mercenaries make in combat, then *Gloomsprinter* is a good option. They can still play out their romance, but the system won't have any rules for falling in love.

If Rebecca and Sanjay are more interested in romance, *Gloomsprinter* has the potential to get in the way of their experience. Hyperfocus on missions and combat means long stretches of play between scenes about intimacy; almost none of the information on *Gloomsprinter* character sheets will be relevant. In this scenario, *Crossed Stars* is the better choice and will allow Rebecca and Sanjay to focus on the stuff that really holds their interest.

Understanding your objectives will help you evaluate how your chosen system supports or inhibits your game. Finding a game that fits your objectives will make playing easier and more fun.

Tone

For narrative play, it's especially important to make sure your group agrees on a **tone**. Tone describes the general style of a story. It affects the content as well as how that content is presented. The same basic premise can make a wildly different experience depending on the tone.

Let's look at how a change in tone might alter the content and presentation of events in a Western:

- **Light, cartoony:** *You shoot at Pigsty Pete and his gang of outlaws as they run out of town. "Yeeeeeouch!" Pete pops ten feet into the air grabbing a hole blown in the back of his pants. "I guess Pigsty Pete won't walk into this town again," the sheriff says with a wink.*
- **Gritty, realistic:** *The air rings with the crack of your revolver. Pigsty Pete falls to the ground with a choking cry. His companions rush to haul him away. You can see blood pooling under his leg. "Looks like Pigsty Pete won't walk in this town again," the sheriff says with a wink that sends chills down your spine. You struggle to holster your revolver, as your hands haven't stopped shaking.*

- **Over the top, action:** *We enter bullet-time and follow your shot through the air. Orchestral music plays while the doves sitting between you and Pete take flight. We can see Pete reflected in the silver coating on your bullet just before it hits him. We resume normal speed as Pigsty Pete's leg explodes in a fountain of blood. Pete screams a string of curses. "I guess Pigsty Pete won't walk in this town again," the sheriff says with a wink, casually taking a drag on his cigar.*

This is the same event, a successful attack against Pigsty Pete. It looks very different based on the tone of the game. Some players would jump at the chance to describe over-the-top gore and violence, while others would rather focus on the emotional impact of taking a life. For some groups killing an antagonist isn't appropriate at all.

Some players can be flexible and move between different tones. Other players might have limitations on tone, based on personal comfort. Finding the right tone will enable your group to invest themselves confidently in the material.

Genre

Genres are stylistic groups that separate fiction into different categories. They are composed of related tropes and setting elements. Working within one or more genres will help your group establish stylistic parameters.

Fantasy adventure might place you in a medieval world full of magic and swordplay, period noir sets you in a stylized vision of the past full of crime and betrayal, and modern-day slice of life puts you in a grounded world like our own. Each of those genres comes with tropes that have major implications for the sort of content we expect to see, and those will dictate the stylistic feel of the game.

Depending on which genre you choose, the same setting can feel dramatically different. Let's say we want to play a game set in space where characters can travel between worlds. Lots of genres can support that setting, but they each can look very different:

- **Far future sci-fi:** Technology is incredibly advanced and not limited by what we understand to be possible. There are a vast number of intelligent aliens to interact with, and space is open to explore with some kind of faster-than-light transportation.
- **Near-future hard sci-fi:** Technology is familiar; this genre might use concepts we have imagined but not built. A character's reach is restricted to our solar system, and alien life is more scientifically grounded. Probably no faster-than-light travel.
- **Sci-fi pulp:** A retro take on space with streamlined rockets and bubble helmets. Aliens look like humans in cheap costumes or bug-eye green monsters with ray guns. Lasers, rockets, and crystals reflect marvelous, but not scientifically realistic, technology.
- **Space punk:** Technology is advanced, but most of what PCs have access to is old and clunky. There are no aliens, but humans give you more than enough to worry about. Long-distance space travel is controlled by oppressive entities.
- **Space opera:** Not only is technology wildly advanced, but it's been that way for a long time. Things don't have to scientifically make sense, and there can even be a touch of magic and mysticism. Aliens are all over the place. Faster-than-light travel is commonplace.
- **Dying Earth:** Interplanetary technology is new, experimental, or rare. All of humanity is forced onto a small fleet or a single ship.

Depending on which of these genres you choose, the aesthetics and attitude of your setting will change. Genre will also likely have an influence on the kind of stories and characters your group creates. The youngest in a long line of space princes is probably not a good concept for space punk or near-future sci-fi, but that adventure would be right at home in space opera or sci-fi pulp.

MIX AND MATCH
In RPGs we also have the ability to blend and remix genres to create new conventions. Combining genres can expand the narrative tools and aesthetics available to players and even sharpen the focus of the game.

Try adding one of these subgenres to one of the genres just discussed to create a more focused vision for our space-faring game:

- Western
- Mecha
- Horror

- Superhero
- Slice of Life
- Noir

Combining space opera with mecha lets us know that most of the conflict is going to revolve around pilots battling with anthropomorphic robot suits. The scale of battle will be immense, and the mechs don't need to follow a grounded logic. Mixing mecha with space punk will lower the scale of combat. There could be a huge galactic war in the background, but protagonists in a mecha space punk story will likely be a small family trying to keep their rusting machines together so they can survive.

Genre provides a stylistic architecture to frame your game. It will help players make similar assumptions, which is one of your major goals for stating objectives.

Story and Character Goals

Once you've established the larger objectives, it's still good to have an explicit discussion about what everyone wants to do with those concepts. Even if players aren't sure where their PCs are going to end up, they probably have a general idea of the direction they want to head. The GM can also establish goals for the game with the group. If the group knows the GM wants to run an adventure in a hollow Earth, they're less likely to try to avoid a cave that will take them there.

THE SPOILER TRAP FOR GMs

Some players are afraid to discuss their ideas because they want to avoid spoilers for the group. This is really tricky territory. As we've discussed, your fellow players *are* an audience, but they are also your creative partners. Playing your ideas too close to your chest can confuse or even alienate your collaborators. You might even find it difficult or frustrating to move your story forward because no one knows how to help you tell the story.

Let's say your GM asks everyone to create soldiers for a military campaign. Your character is Li Cheng, a private who aspires to advance in rank so he can feel closer to veterans he admires in his family. However, by session two, it's clear that your party is meant to desert their mission. Knowing that, you might have created a different character.

Stories are flexible. It would definitely be interesting to watch Cheng adjust to a new reality, but that doesn't necessarily mean you're interested in exploring *that*. The early twist of having to desert *could* be a fun surprise, but not if the most engaging aspects of your character disappear. You can avoid potential disappointment by discussing general concepts in terms of your objective for the game.

As a player you can state, "I want to see this character advance in a military career." This establishes that both you and your character are interested in exploring that story. It sets a kind of boundary specific to the character concept. If the GM's story doesn't have room for a plot like that, it gives them an opportunity to let you know your initial concept won't fit.

Alternatively, the GM could decide their plot isn't totally incompatible with your desire to play a military hero. If they know your objective for Cheng, they have the opportunity to assure you there is room for your story even if the plot seems like it's going in another direction. Responding with "Are you open to your character taking a nontraditional path toward that goal?" lets you know that surprises might be in store, but it doesn't let you know what they are. When the twist pops up, you are free to lean into what's happening because you know your GM has acknowledged your objective.

THE SPOILER TRAP FOR PCs

Some character plots revolve around hidden information. It's tempting to keep your fellow PCs in the dark to set up a big reveal.

PCs have less responsibility for your personal story than the GM, so treating them more like an audience makes sense. However, without knowing what you want for your story, it's difficult for your fellow players to understand your choices. The last thing you want is to frustrate your friends while setting up a fun surprise.

Let's say you're playing Requiem Signal, a mercenary who used to work for the game's primary antagonist. Requiem has a kill switch implanted in their neck, and they need to deactivate it before they can truly be free.

Your preference might be to reveal this information at a dramatic moment. If your fellow PCs don't know that, they could push to confront the villain before you're ready, robbing your moment of its impact. They might become frustrated with you for resisting what seems like an obvious plan, or blame the GM for preventing them from achieving a simple goal.

Telling your group, "I need to confront the villain before I take revenge," lets them know your objective requires you to have some kind of direct conversation. It will prevent confusion from tearing the group apart.

Providing an even more specific objective empowers the group to actively support your story. Saying, "My character has a secret she is hesitant to share, but she trusts this group to help her confront the villain before getting revenge," keeps your secret but lets the group know you have one. This way when you're dramatically cagey they can play along. They can also assume your character's surprising behavior is related to an impending plot twist and not a lack of cooperation.

Generally speaking, your fellow players want to work with you to have fun. It's hard for them to do that if they don't know the kind of fun you want to have. Setting objectives brings all of that into the open, empowering everyone to work together.

Story- or System-Led Creation

It's possible to tell stories with no formal rules at all. Role-playing systems help to make the process easier by creating a structural foundation everyone agrees upon. There are two major approaches to utilizing game systems to create a narrative, *system-led* and *story-led*. In this chapter, we'll explore the philosophy behind both approaches and how they interact with narrative differently.

System-Led Creation

System-led creation allows the rules of a game system to take the lead in shaping your story. It works by players supporting and justifying the results of mechanical interactions.

Let's say we're playing an RPG about rock and roll. PCs are rock stars trying to make it big. Our game has four **stats**: Strength, Skill, Style, and Hair.

KNOW YOUR STATS

For our rock RPG the basic statistics that make up a PC are as follows:

- Strength: Raw physical power and ability to lift heavy equipment.
- Skill: Actual musical talent and performance ability.
- Style: The sum of a star's looks and personality that creates a personal mystique.
- Hair: How noticeable and distinct their haircut is.

To create a character, players roll a six-sided die (d6) to randomly assign a value to each stat, with 1 being least powerful and 6 being most powerful.

Roll a d6 to Make Your Rock Star

○ Strength ....   ○ Style ....

○ Skill ....   ○ Hair ....

Based on your rolls, what kind of rock star do you have? A 1 in Strength might mean you have a performer who doesn't really work out; a 5 might make them a powerlifter who also plays music. A 2 in Style might mean this performer typically blends in with the general population, while 4 means they act and dress eccentrically. Getting 6 in Hair could give them a brash iconic haircut, or maybe it means they're some kind of guitar-playing Sasquatch.

We can create a story about who this character is just by interpreting the numbers we rolled. That interpretation helps us make assumptions about the character's looks, personality, and backstory.

SYSTEM-LED CREATION FOR PCs

Lots of games lean on system-led character creation. Some games don't offer players many choices, generating characters and their traits entirely through random rolls. Games like this are largely disinterested in character stories that don't evolve out of play. Others use randomization to simulate certain character traits being rare within the game world—for instance, a system that only allows players to select "Mech Pilot" as their character class if they randomly roll the correct combination of abilities at character creation.

It's also possible to use a system-led approach in games that provide players with lots of options. Some players have fun mechanically optimizing characters to give them specialized strengths. Others view this so-called power-gaming approach as detrimental to narrative play. However, prioritizing game mechanics doesn't have to mean disregarding story value. It just decides your order of operations. It can be rewarding to justify how bizarre combinations of abilities came to be.

As always, the choice of what to invest in a character is up to the player. Some players relish the opportunity to interpret and justify nonsensical character traits; others just want the tools they need to engage with the game.

SYSTEM-LED CREATION FOR GMs

GMs can take a system-led approach to running games, allowing randomizers to determine the type, difficulty, and reward for challenges encountered by the PCs. Approaching games this way makes the GM role more reactive. The GM in this case is mostly responsible for making sense of random events and managing player responses to them.

Alternatively a GM can engage in system-led creation by using published adventure modules. These are game scenarios created by RPG publishers and fans. They provide the GM with NPCs, locations, challenges, and storylines they can use to run a game. **Modules** still need the GM to bring the story to life, but game materials in a module have a much stronger influence on how that story unfolds.

It's also system-led creation to take inspiration from a single game concept and build a story around it. For example, let's say you're the GM and you decide you want to see your party face a dragon. The stats and description for a dragon inspire the game, but most of the story burden is on you. You have to give your players a motivation to fight the dragon, guide them to its lair, decide what that environment is like, and control the dragon during the fight.

Story-Led Creation

Story-led creation is starting with an idea for a narrative, then adapting your idea into the system. Some players come up with ideas for stories or characters without knowing what game they want to play. Some players like to take the same basic character and play them in different games. Everyone approaching RPGs this way is engaging in story-led creation.

To illustrate this type of narrative creation, let's return to our rock star RPG. This time we're going to start with a concept for a rock star and use the tools available in the game to accurately reflect them. Picture a rock star in your mind. Make your own, or choose an existing performer. Then return to the stats we used earlier. Instead of rolling a die, this time we start with a total of 10 points to distribute among our four stats. Assign points to Strength, Skill, Style, and Hair, trying to reflect your concept as best you can:

✹ Assign 10 Points to Make Your Rock Star

O Strength ------------   O Style ------------

O Skill ------------   O Hair ------------

EXAMPLE: AGAMEMNON LA PERRIER
Lumberjack by day, bassist by night. His day job as a lumberjack requires lots of raw physical strength, and life in northern Canada

has driven him to cultivate a large beard and body hair to stay warm. Agamemnon is more enthusiastic than talented, and you probably wouldn't be able to tell the difference between him and your average lumberjack just by looking at him. As a result, he has a 4 in both Strength and Hair, and a 1 in Skill and Style.

EXAMPLE: COSMIC REA

For story-led creation we're focused on using the tools a game gives us to represent an idea. It's possible to have an idea larger than the constraints the mechanics allow. Let's say we want to make a glam rocker, Cosmic Rea, who could justifiably be represented by a 5 in Skill, Style, and Hair.

The example game only allows players to assign 10 points to character stats though. In this case, we have to evaluate how to pursue our objective outside the standard framework. Maybe your group can change the rules to allow more points to better represent the concept. Your group could agree that the stats reflect a different scale that only applies to rock stars. Rea's hair might be impressive compared to a normal person, but for rock stars, it only registers at a 1 or a 2.

You can also adjust your concept according to the constraints of the system. "Story-led" simply means story ideas are taking the lead in how a concept is formed. You can always alter your initial idea to better fit the rules. Maybe we're seeing Cosmic Rea early in their career before they had the money to support their magnificent Style and Hair.

STORY-LED CREATION FOR PCs

Story-led creation is popular for players who have a strong vision of what they want out of a game. It usually works best with systems that place a heavy emphasis on narrative solutions, or mechanically oriented games with a large variety of options. A game needs to be flexible to accommodate the limitless potential of creativity.

When creating characters with a story-led approach it's important to think of a game system as a medium for expressing creativity. Expression is rarely a complete process. Even an amazing piece by a very talented artist is limited by the scope of the medium with which it was created.

If you were to draw your character, you'd be confined by the realities of that medium. It's not possible to accurately color an image of an alien that comes in colors beyond the visible spectrum. Similarly, a game might only have rules to represent a fraction of the ideas that make up your character concept. Even if all the options exist, you might not be able to fit all of your plans into one character. Sometimes story-led creation is a matter of focusing on what you feel is most important and sacrificing other aspects to get at the heart of what you want.

Story-led creation can also be fun for folks who really enjoy expressing themselves through game rules. There are communities of players who work to make versions of their favorite fictional characters in different RPGs. With their story-led creativity they might try to make a version of Robin Hood using a horror mystery game or a cosmic space opera.

STORY-LED CREATION FOR GMs

A story-led approach will place a heavier creative burden on you when you are the GM, but in exchange for your efforts you are allowed to put more of yourself into the game. As a GM you can create entire worlds. Games give you the tools to structure that kind of creativity. For some GMs, story-led creation is what draws them to the role. Others only try to approach games this way after developing a sense of comfort with the role.

On a very basic level, the GM's role is driven by story-led creation. Every time you ask players to make a roll, or simply respond to their questions, you are making a judgment on when the events of the narrative warrant interaction with the game's rules.

Here's an example. Joquan is running an espionage game. His party plans to distract and sneak past a security guard. Joquan has all sorts of options to respond to this plan:

- He could call for his players to roll for both distraction and stealth to see how every aspect of implementing this plan affects the overall scene.

- He could decide the stealth check is the most important aspect of the plan and only require a roll for that. He can represent the distraction as a bonus to the stealth roll.
- He also has the power to decide that the security guard isn't worth focusing on and just say the party makes it past.

In all these examples Joquan is using story-led creation by turning the narrative information of "my party plans to sneak past this guard" into mechanical actions related to the game's rules.

Representing information through game mechanics draws a special kind of attention to its importance in the story. If Joquan takes the time to stat out his security guard NPC, the players will have more options to interact with that character in game terms.

Knowing the guard's skills and hit points allows the party to fully engage with the character through the combat system. Without that information, Joquan is limited in how faithfully he can represent certain player choices. We'll cover this concept more when we discuss text in Chapter 5, but for now, it's important to know that mechanics are a way to highlight story information. Choosing where you apply mechanics affects the options every player has for using the game.

This is true for aspects of play that have nothing to do with game mechanics as well. If Joquan takes the time to give his security guard an emotional state or backstory, it changes the party's options once again. It makes a difference if the security guard is an off-duty cop supplementing his income with a part-time job, or a nineteen-year-old kid who was an athlete in high school.

When you take a story-led approach to GMing, your role becomes much larger. Understanding the ways the GM role is inherently story-led will help you challenge assumptions about what needs to happen in your games and gives you greater control.

All player choices are important enough for Joquan to respond to, but based on his group's objective he can choose how best to honor those ideas in the spirit of the game. Broadly speaking he can represent choices in the following ways:

- **Initiative-based action:** This means slowing down game time to moment-to-moment beats where each player contributes to the scene in turn order. It pulls the focus of the entire game into a single event.
- **Skill roll:** A single PC tests their character's abilities against a task to see if it will succeed or fail; either result drives the story forward.
- **Bonus/setback:** A PC action or game world condition is represented as a significant component of a larger action.
- **Pure narration:** Player contributions are brought into the reality of the fiction through narration but don't interact with game mechanics.

✷ **Select an objective for a style of play for this espionage game:**
- O Tactical, realistic
- O Campy, over the top
- O Self-serious action adventure
- O Parody

✷ **Based on the objective you selected, how do you think Joquan should represent the following story events?**
- O A PC attacks the security guard to steal their uniform.
- O A PC hacks a computer terminal.
- O The guard gets up from his desk to use the bathroom.
- O A PC throws a pen to distract the guard.
- O A PC attempts to seduce the guard.
- O A PC picks the lock on a door.
- O One PC has an argument with another about the plan.

✎ Does your choice change when the group's objective changes?

The information you choose to represent mechanically and through backstory can all be framed through your group's objective. If Joquan's players agree that they want a tactical experience, then it probably makes sense for him to stat the guard or generally be prepared for the party to interact with an NPC mechanically. If the group's objective is to play a campy James Bond–esque campaign, Joquan should avoid making the character pose too much of an individual threat. Ultra-competent superspies shouldn't be daunted by a rent-a-cop.

Session Zero

Some players like to set aside time to discuss their game, characters, and world before the first official instance of role-playing. This technique is called a **Session Zero**. It gives players an opportunity to establish objectives, provide the GM with plot hooks, and create a foundation for character relationships. A Session Zero is never compulsory, but it makes narrative gaming *much* easier. This chapter is a short guide to walking your group through a Session Zero.

Preparing to Prepare

Before you sit down to a Session Zero we recommend establishing a few things with the group first:

- **Genre:** You'll explore the details of what this means during Session Zero, but even a general idea of genre helps a group establish common ground. Something like fantasy, Western, noir, or cyberpunk should be enough to get people started.
- **Game system:** Picking an RPG lets players know what tools they'll have for role-play and channels character concepts into more focused categories.
- **Setting:** If you are working with an established setting or one that is possible to research, letting people know before Session Zero helps them bring more relevant ideas to the table. If you have no setting, it lets people know they can bring general character concepts to refine.

- **Scenario:** Establish if there is a specific premise for the game like "robbing a bank," "fighting crime in a city," or "hunting for a mole."
- **Power level:** Lots of RPGs have character progression mechanics. A level 1 character looks very different from a level 6 or level 15 character.
- **Expected length of game:** The number of sessions a game is intended to run impacts the type of character and world concepts players can expect to explore. A game that runs one to three sessions needs fully formed characters to play off a focused scenario. A long campaign can accommodate unformed characters with long-term goals and has the freedom to explore several aspects of a setting.

Establishing these facts before Session Zero focuses players. Creating a few limitations actually makes it easier to generate ideas. You don't need to answer all of these questions, but the more you do, the greater the chance people will have compatible ideas.

Step 1: Establish Genre and Tone

Genre and tone have a dramatic impact on the ideas people generate in-game. The first step of setting your objective is getting everyone to speak the same narrative language.

GENRE

Specifying a genre, such as fantasy, doesn't do enough to establish an objective. The Lord of the Rings, *Game of Thrones*, and The Chronicles of Narnia series are all fantasy and they each feel very different.

To define what a given genre means to your group discuss the following questions:

- What is your favorite aspect of the game we chose?
- What's your favorite aspect of the setting?
- What books, films, comics, or TV shows in this genre inspire you?
- What would you like to see in this game based on our genre?

- What do you like about the ideas other players brought to the table?
- What do you find less interesting?

This will help foster a common understanding among players of what your genre actually means. It gives everyone an opportunity to build on a foundation that they agree upon in the open. Any tropes can be avoided or integrated before people invest time and creativity.

TONE

Tone is sometimes one of the underlying assumptions people make when they pick a genre. However, genre is really too subjective to rely on unspoken agreements, especially when it has a dramatic impact on the content of a game. To create an understanding for tone, the group should discuss at least a few key subjects, including violence; gender, romance, and sexuality; and comedy and drama.

VIOLENCE

Violence is present in many RPGs, and it can take many different forms. In the US people are exposed to depictions of violence in all sorts of media, which means it's possible to maintain a specific comfort level surrounding the subject.

During your Session Zero, use the following questions to help guide your discussion about violence:

- Based on our discussion of genre, what is the role of violence in our story?
  - Is it simply a way to frame action scenes?
  - Do characters emotionally react to violence perpetrated by themselves or others?
- How much do we want to explore specific actions in combat?
  - Will players go into detail beyond "I punch" or "I slash"?
  - Are we okay hearing about blood, injury, and gore?
- How realistic do we want to be with the violence we depict?
  - How long do we want to spend recovering from injuries?
  - Are we prepared to see tragedy resulting from violent action?

- Will PCs fear or use violence?
- In a horror game violence might be a tool of fear. In fantasy adventure, it's how people make a living. How does that change our perception?
- Is there a moral judgment placed on violence?

SELF-AWARENESS

RPGs have a history of otherizing certain groups like orcs, vampires, or enemy nations to justify killing them to take their stuff. Historically, this behavior perpetrated against real people has led to some terrible crimes. It's up to the group to determine how the game will approach these subjects. Being aware of harmful attitudes and stereotypes allows you to actively choose what you want to explore.

GENDER, ROMANCE, AND SEXUALITY

Many people grow up with limited tools for discussing intimacy. There are plenty of groups who will feel more comfortable discussing beheading than kissing. Pop culture generally has an uncomfortable history with gender and sexuality; many games were inspired by stories that perpetuate harmful tropes. What some players might see as standard aspects of a setting could be harmful or uncomfortable for others.

These questions will help ensure that the members of your group are on the same page when it comes to this important aspect of your game's tone:

- Is there oppression based on gender and sexuality in this world?
  - Are we interested in struggling against oppression or would we rather ignore it?
  - How vulnerable might our PCs be to oppression if they encounter it?

- ▸ Could gender and sexuality be viewed differently in a fantasy world?
- Do we want to see romance in this game?
  - ▸ If so, are we comfortable with PCs being in relationships with other PCs, or should we restrict romance to NPCs?
  - ▸ Are there any game mechanics that should be off-limits when dealing with romance and intimacy?
  - ▸ Are there mechanics we want to incorporate to make intimacy approachable?
- How do we want to deal with sex?
  - ▸ What sort of physical intimacy are we comfortable seeing?
  - ▸ When should the game cut away?
  - ▸ Do we have a way of easily voicing discomfort?

SAFETY FIRST

A few game designers have designed mechanics that can be incorporated into any game to help players communicate around uncomfortable subjects and maintain boundaries that keep the game fun. Here are a few you might want to look up:

- The X-Card by John Stavropoulos
- Lines and Veils by Emily Care Boss
- Script Change by Brie Beau Sheldon
- The Support Flower by Tayler Stokes
- The OK Check-In recommended iteration by Maury Brown, Sarah Lynne Bowman, and Harrison Greene

COMEDY AND DRAMA

A big part of tone is how seriously your group addresses events in the story. Some groups are happy to lean into intense emotions and high drama; others want to blow off steam and do wild things without consequences. It's possible to tell great stories no matter how you approach the game, but mismatched expectations will lead to frustration.

These discussion points will help clarify your group's attitudes concerning comedy and drama:

- How seriously are we taking this game? What is our attitude regarding its events?
  - ▸ Is this an artistic and personal story?
  - ▸ Are we comfortable with emotional exploration?
  - ▸ Will we treat certain aspects like a competition?
- When can/should we joke at the table?
  - ▸ In or out of character whenever we want?
  - ▸ In character as long as it fits the scene?
  - ▸ Only after we have resolved dramatic moments?
- What sort of drama and humor are we comfortable with?
  - ▸ Are there any subjects that should be off-limits?
  - ▸ Are we comfortable exploring real-world subjects through fantasy?
  - ▸ What do we do if our game crosses a line for someone?

Step 2: Collaborate On a Setting

After figuring out the basics an optional step is to have players collaborate on creating details about the setting. Some players like to treat the world as the sole domain of the GM. However, opening up this responsibility to the group during Session Zero gives everyone a chance to add something they find interesting. It's a really helpful activity for getting players to invest.

LOCATIONS

Cities, structures, and even landmarks are a great place to start. Places help establish a sense of what is possible in a setting. A world with cities built onto the backs of gigantic turtles will feel very different from a world where people are forced to live in sealed domes connected by tubes.

Have each player answer at least one of these questions:

- What natural landmark inspires awe?
- What structure is shrouded in mystery?
- What is the most dangerous town to live in?
- Where would you travel to find something rare?
- What place reminds you of the real world?
- Is this world an unusual shape?
- What place is untamed by civilization?
- Where would someone hide a valuable treasure?
- Where would a traveler go to relax?
- What place or thing do people make pilgrimages to visit?
- Where do people seek knowledge?
- What's an exciting place by the sea to visit?
- Where is it treacherous to travel?

PEOPLE

Every game needs a good cast of NPCs! Characters help make a world feel alive. When PCs establish their own allies, rivals, and antagonists they give the GM easy tools with which to draw them in.

Have each player answer at least one of these questions:

- Who is undeniably more powerful than your party?
- What dangerous organization might your character deal with cautiously?
- Who does your character respect?
- If you burned most of your bridges, who would you turn to for help?
- Who guards secrets that you might want to know?
- Which organization is useful enough to make up for being occasionally inconvenient?
- Who is the most respected leader your character can think of?
- Who controls a great deal of power behind the scenes?
- Which antagonistic group is more complicated than it appears?
- Which organization supports the arts?
- What gang, tribe, or faction is just fun to hang out with?

RUMORS AND MYSTERIES

Rumors and mysteries are useful storytelling tools. When PCs create rumors and mysteries, they make their ideas influential but unreliable. Depending on what the GM likes, they could be establishing hard truths, getting select details wrong, or creating widely believed lies.

Have each player answer at least one of these questions:

- What threat goes by many names?
- Which living figure do some believe to be dead?
- Which dead figure do some believe to be alive?
- How does the sun rise and fall?
- What ruin defies explanation?
- What natural event seems to conflict with our understanding of nature?
- What lost treasure has claimed the lives of many who sought it?
- Why do travelers avoid strangers?
- What happens to items that seem to disappear?
- Who has been betrayed but does not know it?
- What great threat waits to be awakened?
- What skill provides mysterious power?
- Where does one seek unknowable truth?

Step 3: Define Your Characters

It's time to introduce your main cast of PCs! You can do this before or during the creation of details about your setting. Doing it afterward helps players understand the boundaries of the world better and allows them to mold their characters to match the game world.

It's a good idea to allow the work you do in Session Zero to influence your character. It will make it easier for you to navigate the story. This could mean showing up with a mostly blank slate, a work in progress, or a willingness to make adjustments after Session Zero is over.

CONCEPT

It's helpful to start with a strong summary. Ideally, you want to touch on the major aspects of your character in one to three sentences. There will be time to fill in details as your conversation unfolds and as you play. Providing too much information right away will actually make it harder for your fellow players to understand your character.

SUMMARY

EXAMPLE
Sherlock Holmes: A consulting detective who uses his intellect and knowledge of London to solve difficult cases. He's brash and doesn't keep to certain social conventions, which causes him to clash with certain people. He has a close friend in his partner, Dr. John Watson.

GOALS
Stating charter goals explicitly establishes what you are interested in seeing your character do. Having this written down will help your collaborators understand how to support the kind of game you want

to play. The more people know what you want, the more they can help you get there. In certain cases, you might feel compelled to share goals only with your GM. That's totally fine; as long as you are sharing with someone, you're making it easier to play the way you want.

Goals should be simple enough to express in a sentence or two. To make it easier we've divided goals into three categories: Small, Medium, and Large. Small goals are simple tasks that can be completed in a single session or that you return to occasionally. Medium goals take effort and usually need devoted focus or a handful of game sessions to complete. Large goals are huge character arcs that might take you a dozen sessions or even a whole campaign to pursue.

Goals can be things your character wants *or* things you want for your character. Think of them as moments that make you more invested in the story. Assigning goals a status of Small, Medium, or Large also signals how difficult you want them to be to create a satisfying arc.

Small:

Medium:

Large:

EXAMPLE
Sherlock Holmes

🖊 **Small:**

Gain the upper hand on Inspector Lestrade with a devastatingly witty line. Wear a disguise to get information. Find a detail everyone else overlooked.

🖊 **Medium:**

Ensure Dr. Watson's new fiancée does not disrupt the lifestyle to which I have become accustomed. Uncover the identity of the Crimson Scarf Killer.

🖊 **Large:**

Grow to a level of emotional maturity that will allow my friend to be happy.

RELATIONSHIPS

Once everyone has established their core character traits, the final step is establishing relationships between PCs. Most games try to keep a party together. It requires much less narrative gymnastics if PCs invest in one another.

To help clarify player relationships, have each PC answer one of these questions for at least two of their companions:

- What do you have to teach this person?
- What do you wish to learn from this person?
- Why do you feel indebted to this person? How do you prefer to pay?

- Why does this person owe you a great debt? How do you wish to collect?
- What do you refuse to admit about this person?
- How does this person make you feel uniquely at ease?
- Why does your personality cause you to clash with this person?
- What great mystery are you trying to unravel about this person?
- What great destiny do you desire for this person?
- What deed by this person has won your respect, if not your loyalty?
- What recurring dream does this person play a part in?
- What is the common scar you share with this person?
- How does fate keep drawing you and this person together?
- What kind of relationship do you aspire to have with this person?
- You suspect this person favors your company—why?
- What about this person makes you nervous?
- How has this person fooled you? Why do you want to believe it?
- How does this person make you feel strong?
- Who in your party would you pass the gates of hell for?
- You have worked with this person before; what about that experience makes you trust them now?
- What secret do you trust this person to keep?
- You feel sorry for this person; why do you seek to ease their pain?
- You are often exhausted by this person; why are they still indispensable to you?
- What lie do you live for the sake of this companion? Is there a potential it will become truth?
- You consider this person a part of your family; how did you solidify that bond?
- One companion knows you harbor hidden feelings for another; how did they find out?
- What makes you trust this person when you have never trusted anyone like them before?

EXAMPLE
Sherlock Holmes

Companion: Dr. John Watson

🖉 **How does this person make you feel uniquely at ease?**
For the sake of those without keen powers of
intuition, I speak my observations aloud as I work.
Since John has become my partner, I speak mostly
for his benefit. It never occurred to me how alone
I was with my thoughts.

Companion: Irene Adler

🖉 **What deed by this person has won your respect, if not your loyalty?**
Irene has bested me once as I discovered her
deception too late. I know her well enough not to
trust her, but I have much to learn from her.

Companion: Inspector Lestrade

🖉 **What do you refuse to admit about this person?**
At times a man possessed of dutiful loyalty who is
able to command respect is just as valuable to the
law as a man of great intellect. I rely on Lestrade,
more than he will ever know.

Understanding Text

RPGs revolve around what you say and how you say it. The conversation you have with your fellow players shapes the game world and how events in it unfold. The strength of your narrative depends on your ability to communicate.

Folks who enjoy actual play often credit the GMs and players as "creative geniuses," "amazing actors," and "gifted storytellers." There is definitely an element of truth to those compliments. However, sometimes that admiration can make you doubt your own abilities. It's easy to assume something is beyond your ability when you don't understand it or even have the words to explain it.

What makes actual play performers and RPG players really good is just that they are familiar with a particular type of communication. They've internalized techniques that help viewers and fellow players understand the story they see in their heads. Understanding how stories are told will help you practice more effectively. Eventually it will enable you to develop your own style.

The foundation of storytelling is understanding **text** and how to manipulate it. This chapter will explain what *text* means in the context of an RPG and start you on the path toward effectively controlling it.

What Is Text?

In novels, the words written on the page make up the story. Characters, locations, and scenes all come to us based on what an author wrote on the page—the actual text of the book.

It's possible to apply the concept of text to other mediums. In those cases, we refer to it in the abstract. Pictures, panels, and words make up the text in comics. In film and TV, the text is composed of the script, sets, lighting, soundtrack, costumes, and the performances of the actors. In all mediums, text is the material presented to an audience for interpretation.

In RPGs the text is primarily what players say and how they say it. There are other factors like the information on character sheets and results from randomizers like dice. Ultimately all of that information gets run through one or more players to become the "truth" the group agrees upon to move the story forward.

Presentation and Interpretation

Text might seem like a concept so simple that it's not worth pointing out. On some level every player instinctively understands that the game doesn't move without them. You don't need to acknowledge this fact in order to play. However, if your goal is to craft a strong story, approaching what you do with this understanding will help you move the narrative with intention.

All storytelling is shaped by audience interpretation on some level. RPGs—more than any other storytelling medium—change based on audience interpretation. That's because the audience is also writing the story. The audience's interpretation of what *just* happened is always going to affect what is *about* to happen.

As an example of this dynamic, let's look at how changing the text portraying a particular event will impact our understanding of the story:

One person punches another person.

This is pretty bland text, but it still tells a story. However, it's likely that no two readers will walk away with the same interpretation of that scene. We can project all sorts of unnamed facts onto that information and build totally different narratives. The people involved could be professional boxers, drunk partygoers, or children in a schoolyard. This vague text is capable of supporting all of these realities. Let's see how more information changes that:

A person in a white shirt punches another person.

Any interpretation of this scene in which the person throwing the punch was nude is now explicitly unsupported by the text. Giving a character a white shirt is a very small change, but it still narrows what the audience is able to take away from the text. Now that we understand the basic mechanics behind altering text, let's add some real detail:

Captain Mercury's white tank top ripples as he punches Stygian: The Living Blackhole in the face.

So much has changed. Naming characters gives us some idea of our setting. Those names and honorifics are pretty wacky. These could be characters in a space opera or superhero story. The detail of Captain Mercury wearing a white tank top adds a bit of grounding to all of the fantasy that could spin out of that image. Even with the strange names, people still wear tank tops. Knowing the shirt is rippling allows us to picture an unusual amount of force accompanying this blow.

That's just the *explicit information* we get from the new text. Even without having more information about where these two are, new details allow us as an audience to fill in more gaps. The original text could have placed these characters anywhere, but the audience's biases probably grounded the scene. Knowing that this is *Captain Mercury* punching *Stygian: The Living Blackhole* opens up the possibility of exciting new settings that would have been really unlikely in the earlier versions.

Where do you see this taking place? On top of a tall building? On the bridge of a massive starship? Floating in space in front of a backdrop of the dazzling cosmos? The likelihood that you see these two as drunks in a bar or children in a schoolyard drops significantly, even though they haven't been explicitly described otherwise. Let's look at the full text now:

Captain Mercury's tank top ripples with cosmic power as he punches Stygian: The Living Blackhole in the face. The crack of the impact echoes through the cosmos, shaking the orbit of nearby planets. Briefly, the singularity that gives Stygian their power wavers, as light and matter escape, filling the void with the majesty of creation.

USE YOUR WORDS

Take note of the important role that word choice plays in how the text will be interpreted. "Captain Mercury's tank top ripples with cosmic power" sends a very different message than "Captain Mercury punches very hard." The words you choose to include in the text will have an impact on the ideas you ultimately communicate to your audience.

Now we really know what it looked like when Captain Mercury threw the punch, how that punch affected Stygian, and what it did to their immediate environment. The mental picture we have as an audience now includes all sorts of information, some of which we aren't able to fully comprehend as human beings. This blow "shakes the orbits of nearby planets." That's not a phenomenon anyone has a real point of reference for. If it were to happen you probably wouldn't be able to see it, but you can still picture it. Even if the description is beyond the realm of real-world possibility, the detail gives important information about who these characters are and what their struggle looks like.

Every iteration of the text we just examined describes the same event: One character punches another. Adding to the text with selective detail created an increasingly vivid picture of the scene. Critical information allowed us to sharpen our interpretation of these characters immensely. It's likely that readers still have vastly different ideas of who Mercury and Stygian are, but we now agree on important foundational truths that enable us to work together.

This is why the idea of text is so important. The shared narrative of RPGs lives in understanding between players. What your fellow players create in response to your ideas depends on their interpretation of what you say. Everyone at the table has a personal understanding of the events of the game, but other players only have access to information presented in the text. Manipulating that text allows you to guide interpretation actively.

Explicit versus Implicit Reality

Creating new text in an RPG generates both explicit and implicit realities for the game world. The *explicit reality* is the text we defined earlier, the reality you actively generate by defining explicit truths. The *implicit reality* exists as information the audience extrapolates based on the text. These realities work in tandem to create the audience's experience of the story.

The events of a game are the reality of a fictional universe. There are aspects to the world that we don't see but we assume they exist. Focusing on two gunslingers who are facing off in a town square doesn't make other aspects of the world disappear. Presumably, there are townsfolk, a horizon in the distance, and a sun hanging overhead even if we're not focused on them.

At any given moment in a game, there is too much happening for any person to fully describe it all. For example, our standoff has two characters. Even a single person contains more information than anyone could reasonably present. In this scenario, that's doubled. Their clothing, posture, movements, and facial expressions could fill pages with details. Each character also has an internal experience. They are thinking and feeling during this standoff. Their internal reality could inform their external reality. A confident-looking gunslinger might be battling an internal fear, and that tells us something about the character.

Part of the craft of storytelling is striking a balance between explicit and implicit reality. Every storyteller has to choose what to say and what to leave unsaid. In brief, the explicit reality is composed of everything that was stated aloud as part of the text. Implicit reality is an understanding of the world based on the text, but not directly incorporated into it. Storytelling skill develops around understanding how explicit reality changes implicit reality, and how implicit reality affects our perception of explicit reality.

Let's examine that relationship by introducing a new explicit reality to our text and breaking down how it changes our implicit reality: *Two gunslingers face one another in the town square. A crowd of onlookers shouts encouragement to their champion and hurls insults at her opponent.*

We've added a new explicit reality in the onlookers. We know they exist, we know they are shouting, and we know they have a favorite in this conflict. Knowing the crowd is present and shouting takes away the possibility of silence from our implicit reality. Think of how a scene with lots of shouting differs from one full of tense silence.

Of course, that change is mostly aesthetic. The crowd is cheering *for* one character and *against* another. We can assume that one of these gunslingers represents the interests of a community of people. That explicit reality helps us assign identity roles to these previously neutral characters, building out implicit reality.

Implicit reality is changeable and inconsistent. It changes as we introduce unchanging information to the text. However, implicit reality still affects how we process new explicit information. If we learn that one gunslinger smiles and waves while the other curses, it's going to lead us to see one as the champion and the other as the villain.

EXPLICIT ACKNOWLEDGMENT AND NARRATIVE SIGNIFICANCE

The crowd becomes important to our scene once they are introduced in the text. From a realistic perspective, the onlookers were always a part of the world. However, if they don't appear in the text, their existence is insignificant from the point-of view of the story. Introducing them to the text brings them into the story as critical participants. If they really didn't matter, we wouldn't bother to mention them.

Focus and Perspective

The text tells us more than just what happens in a scene; it tells us *how* it happens and even how to feel about it. When you're rooting for a protagonist, or against an antagonist, it's because the story guided you to that perspective. It showed you things about the protagonist you like and things about the antagonist you don't. We develop relationships with the information in the text based on how it guides our *focus* and *perspective*.

FOCUS

The focus is *where* the text directs our attention. Think of it as the camera in movies and TV. Focus controls where the audience gets its information about the narrative. It tells a larger story by presenting specific shots. It's both the scene directly in front of the audience and what the larger story is about.

Let's return to our gunslinger example:

Sweat beads on the sheriff's brow as the cheers of the crowd pound in her ears, each one a call for help. Her hand trembles, hovering just above the revolver at her side.

The new passage puts focus on just one character. Focusing on the sheriff fills this moment with tension, anxiety, and a sense of purpose. It's possible to interpret that based on earlier passages, but this focus makes some of that meaning explicit.

Shifting focus draws the audience's attention to different information, altering their experience of the story:

The outlaw glances over the raging mob. Their shouts blur into an indistinct drone. He smirks at his opponent and waits for the signal to draw.

The anxiety of the sheriff's story isn't present in the outlaw's. The crowd means nothing to him and he is not afraid. His confidence and detachment tell us something about who he is though. It still moves the story forward even without steeping in the tension present in the sheriff.

PERSPECTIVE

So far, our focus has been on the gunslingers, but their perspective has not come into play. We encounter perspective when a character's knowledge, experience, and personality affect the way the audience interprets the text.

Through the din of the crowd, Zara watches her wife, the sheriff, prepare to draw. She recognizes the look in her wife's eyes. Her hands might shake, but her gaze never wavers when she's found a target.

From Zara's perspective, we still get a hint of the tension our sheriff is feeling. We also get insights about the sheriff that we can't get just by looking at her as a neutral observer. In fact, we couldn't get this information even with perspective information from the sheriff because it depends on her wife's assessment of her character.

PERSPECTIVE AND AGENCY

Most players expect total authority over their character's actions, thoughts, and feelings. When incorporating a character that another player controls into your narration, it's always best to ask for permission and check in to ensure their vision matches your own.

At the gaming table, we have considerable freedom to shift focus and perspective to suit the needs of our scene. Ideally, the text reflects the information you feel is most important about events in your game. As a player in any role, you have a wide range of options when it comes to presenting events in ways that best suit your needs.

Atmosphere

One of the most basic and essential roles the text plays is cultivating *atmosphere*. A story's atmosphere ties directly to the audience's emotional experience. It fluctuates alongside the events of the story to underscore each moment.

A horror story doesn't usually focus on the monster until the final acts. Films about ghosts usually have an hour-long sequence of small objects moving, indistinct figures silhouetted in the background, and weird noises before you see an actual spirit. That's part of an effort to create a spooky atmosphere to prepare the audience for the payoff. Showing the monster too early robs the story of some of its power.

Atmosphere isn't just about setting up future events; it involves presenting material in a way that feels cohesive. Lighting and music changes curate an atmosphere in real time. Soft lights and music usually accompany moments of romance and intimacy, swelling trumpets and bold, bright colors accompany triumph, and discordant music and darkness underscore horror.

Just like in film, you control the atmosphere of your game based on the text present to the audience. That guides the audience's emotional experience of the story and shapes their implicit reality. A well-defined atmosphere helps your collaborators work with you more effectively.

Let's say you're GMing a horror game. Your goal is to curate an atmosphere of uncertainty, danger, and fear. When you describe what the PCs experience, you'll want to highlight aspects of the story that emphasize those feelings. If your party is climbing an old staircase, mentioning that the floorboards creak is a pretty natural choice. It introduces elements to the explicit and implicit reality that add to the atmosphere:

- **Explicit:** This house creaks and groans; the party just made noise; there are unintended consequences for simple actions.
- **Implicit:** The wood is old and may be unreliable. If the party made noise they could be noticed. It will be hard to separate mundane properties of this house from a possible threat.

If the party is in another setting, like a hospital or an office building, atmospheric details you choose in the text could be entirely different. Hospitals have their own horrific atmosphere. Rather than sounds, you might have more success with visual elements like medical equipment or uniforms. Offices offer very little that is inherently horrific, and if the environment isn't doing your atmosphere any favors, then you don't need to focus on it.

ATMOSPHERE AND ACTION

Atmosphere applies to actions as well as environment. Randomizers dictate which actions are successful, but players have ultimate control over how success and failure influence the atmosphere because they choose how to narrate those results.

Let's say our party is fighting a dragon. Playing to different atmospheres changes the text and how it guides our interpretation of the scene:

- **Victorious, empowering:** *Sabo takes advantage of an opening created when the dragon tries to rake him with its claws. With a roll and a slash, Sabo cuts the beast's hide, causing it to snarl in pain.*
- **Subdued, foreboding:** *Sabo's hands ache against the heft of his sword. He knows his blade struck true, but the victory is fleeting. He is struck by how small the wound appears compared to the effort it took to create it.*
- **Personal, emotional:** *The swordmaster spoke of battle as a dance of patience and grace. As an apprentice, Sabo could not appreciate that lesson. Today though, as Sabo dodges and parries the dragon's blows, he feels the rhythm. The dragon is not an obstacle to be broken. It is a partner. Blood flows along the sword; Sabo swings it with grace. In this moment he understands that he has become a master.*
- **Slapstick, comedic:** *Sabo's swearing grows progressively louder as he runs from the frantic slashes of the dragon's claws. He dives behind a boulder and cowers, waving his sword wildly. The*

dragon swipes finish him off, but it stops before he is crushed. Sabo and the dragon make eye contact as they realize Sabo's frantic swings drove his blade into the dragon's claw. The beast and Sabo roar and scream in unison.

All of this narration describes a successful attack, but the atmosphere of each paints a picture of a very different battle.

Using your chosen atmosphere as a goal, you can shape which details you want to bring into the text. It will lead to more cohesive narration and ultimately stronger storytelling. No matter what your group is like, no matter what game you play, you can always use atmosphere as a guide.

BUILD EXPERIENCE

It's possible to master your craft outside of this framework. Not every skilled player approaches the game with the intention of creating good fiction. Practice plays the biggest role in developing skill.

Awareness of the text enables you to *intentionally* develop your abilities. When you struggle with your narration, or marvel at another player's ability, take a moment to ask yourself, How are we using the text? The answer should help you find a way to learn.

Make Choices Important

Storytelling in RPGs is spontaneous and collaborative. It has a great deal in common with improvisational acting. The line between improv and role-playing is extremely thin. It's not unusual to encounter improv techniques in the text of RPGs or in places that offer role-playing advice. In this chapter, we're going to look at the single most relevant lesson improv has to offer RPGs. No matter how you play, understanding this chapter will help you have a better time playing RPGs and building narrative. With that said, let's look at how to make choices important.

Yes and...

Even if you've never encountered improv before, there is a chance that you've heard of "yes and." It's a philosophy taught in introductory improv classes and corporate workshops, and plastered all over improv theater websites. As a result, it also happens to be the most frequently misinterpreted concept in improv.

BACK TO SCHOOL?

Plenty of people will advise RPG players to take improv lessons. If you're enthusiastic about learning a new skill and adopting a new hobby, go for it! However, you don't *need* improv school to be a good role player. Improv is its own discipline; it can take years to master, and lessons can be expensive.

YES

The "yes" signifies accepting the contributions of your ensemble. In an improv performance there is an implicit agreement that anything said or done by the actors on stage is part of the performance. There are a few practical reasons for this idea.

First, rejecting ideas makes it difficult to create a shared reality. Disagreement over what belongs in a performance—while the performance is ongoing—breeds confusion. Normally when something doesn't belong in a performance, it gets cut before the audience ever sees it. Accepting that everything happening is intentional is a shortcut that lets improvisers sidestep the editorial process and say "It's all here because it's supposed to be."

Second, it makes the whole creative process easier. If you've ever been asked to tell a story out of thin air, you understand how difficult it is to build something out of nothing. Working together spreads the burden of creativity around, but it only works if you actually engage with your partner's ideas. Working together starts with saying "yes."

AND

"And" signifies building on what has been established. Starting with a shaky or insubstantial idea is fine in improv because it's only a small part of a larger picture. Improvisers work together to add to whatever they start with, creating meaning by connecting the dots as they go. Many improv shows start with a random idea shouted from the audience because it doesn't matter what kicks things off as long as everyone keeps building. "And" asks performers to actively contribute. It's not enough to simply accept a fellow performer's ideas; you have to build on them.

It's a deceptively simple methodology: accept what you are given and build on it. Yet it's remarkable how difficult this can be to put into practice. People ignore and actively reject ideas *constantly* without giving it the slightest thought. Engaging as a collaborator is an active choice, and it takes training to make it a habit.

THE IMPORTANCE OF "NO"

Remember when we said that "yes and" is often misinterpreted? Folks just learning improv or only familiarizing themselves with the basics sometimes treat "yes and" as an inflexible guide. Doing this puts performers at risk by limiting their ability to set boundaries.

Accepting and building on ideas doesn't come naturally to most people. We often reject ideas subconsciously. For simplicity's sake, most classes discourage denial—rejecting, ignoring, or otherwise not engaging with the ideas of your fellow performers. If you're trying to learn a skill, it's easy to moralize setbacks and failures. Moralizing all forms of denial as antithetical to progress leads some folks to believe improv shouldn't have boundaries or limitations at all. It also makes some people afraid of "no" as a word, which is ridiculous.

If one character tells another to drink a vial of poison that will instantly kill them, a shaky understanding of "yes and" might lead you to think that there is no choice but to drink. This misinterpretation limits a performer's ability to act authentically and opens the possibility that people will be put in positions they really don't want to be in.

RPGs and improv are limited only by imagination, which means they can enter territory that is challenging or even harmful. Voicing discomfort with that kind of content is *not* a liability. Maintaining boundaries in favor of comfort and safety is actually an asset to the game. It's easier for people to create when they are at ease!

WHAT IS "YES"?

"Yes" means accepting the reality your scene partner establishes, not necessarily acquiescing to the desires of their character. Let's think of this in terms of game scenes.

> **GM:** *You are confronted by a great sphinx outside the Tomb of Delights. It challenges you to a game of riddles to win entry...*

Here, the GM has initiated a few ideas. There is a Tomb of Delights with a great sphinx guarding it. Solving riddles can get the party inside.

The party doesn't *have* to enter the riddle contest though. They can disguise themselves as tomb inspectors to sneak in, fight the sphinx to force their way in, or spend weeks excavating the ground immediately behind the sphinx to dig their way in. These choices still follow the principle of "yes and" because the players have acknowledged that there is a tomb and a sphinx, and if they want to enter the tomb they must get past the sphinx.

Returning to the vial-of-poison example, "yes" is acknowledging the vial exists and that it has been offered. Anything that follows is part of "and." If you choose to have your character refuse to drink, your "and" is "and this scene will be about you trying to convince me to drink it." There are other ways to frame this kind of contribution. Some call it "no and," "yes but," or "no but." In all cases the idea is the same: accept the reality of the scene and build.

"Yes" is really just about creating narrative momentum.

LISTENING

To apply improv lessons to RPGs we need to learn the lesson that follows immediately after "yes and." Improvisers are encouraged to actively listen to each other in order to make "yes and" work. Active listening is more than just hearing what your collaborators are saying. It's thinking about their ideas and searching them for meaning.

If all you're doing while another player is talking is waiting so you can see how you can make *your* next idea make sense, you're not collaborating. Taking the time to examine ideas opens you up to using them in new and exciting ways. Effective collaboration involves searching the explicit reality your fellow players put in the text for compelling implicit reality, then expressing your discovery through new text. This builds the explicit reality by honoring your friends' ideas with attention and creativity.

Passive listening allows the game to work. It does the bare minimum of supporting a basic "yes and" structure. Active listening sets you up to really work together and transforms the game into collaborative art.

Making Choices Important

Many veteran improvisers say the real craft of improv lives in making your scene partner look good. A skilled improviser isn't someone who constantly spouts off clever ideas; it's someone who can turn any idea into something clever. Listening and "yes and" are tools that help you do that. However, the thing that really drives improv as an art is the intent to engage with other people's ideas and add meaning to them. The easiest way to frame this kind of active collaboration is to task yourself with the mission of *making choices important.*

This particular improv lesson separates narrative gaming from other approaches to RPG play. Many people see RPGs as a personally driven experience. As a PC the game they are interested in is about *their* character. As a GM the game is about *their* world. Your only responsibility is cultivating your own experience while trusting everyone else to take care of themselves. There's nothing wrong with approaching RPGs this way. You can still have fun and even tell great stories while you do it.

An individualist perspective makes storytelling harder though. If we're all just throwing out our own ideas and simply acknowledging other contributions, the game moves, but it's not necessarily cohesive or interesting. No matter your role, you still only make up a fraction of the game. If your goal is a strong overall narrative, focusing on just your ideas leaves a lot up to chance. To see how collaboration affects storytelling potential, let's look at an example. Evan and Claire are preparing characters for a fantasy game.

> **Evan:** *I'm a paladin from a holy order of knights sworn to protect these lands from the forces of evil.*

> **Claire:** *I'm a former thief trained by a secretive and shadowy guild with branches across many kingdoms.*

These characters could be fun and interesting and everyone will probably enjoy watching them work together. Right now though, there is nothing linking them. Each player has invested creativity only in their own character. One cool idea and another *unrelated* cool idea don't give us a story. Let's see how things develop when these players make each other's choices important:

Evan: *Cool! The thieves guild is probably something only a few people in my order want to acknowledge. My master cautioned me against chasing waterfalls, but I want to prove myself! Even if it means looking for trouble. I'll be excited at the opportunity to introduce you to the order's way of thinking and learn about your guild.*

Claire: *Yeah, your order is a major concern for the guild. We were taught to be careful around you because you're more than just cops who get tied up in red tape. You need to be at least a little rebellious to be a thief, so it makes sense I immediately sought out an order paladin after quitting. I probably feel safe and exposed at the same time around you.*

With just a little investment we have a potentially interesting and nuanced dynamic for these two. Evan played up the secretive nature of Claire's thieves guild and made learning about it a character goal. Now his character's story will automatically mean learning more about Claire's character's past. Claire played up the paladin order's power and noble intentions, making Evan's concept cooler. She also gave her character a personality that will draw her to Evan's paladin and make them clash. It's automatically more interesting to picture these characters together *and* they have some long-term goals.

That sort of story development can't happen in isolation. Even if the concepts Evan and Claire brought to the table were thoroughly fleshed out, the story of the game is going to revolve around their interaction. Having really robust plot elements that don't overlap pulls the story in different directions. It divides audience interest and makes it harder for everyone to have fun.

If everyone at the table—or even just a few players—is approaching play with the goal of "making choices important," storytelling gets easier and better for everyone.

WHAT MAKES THIS WORK?

Now we understand some of the forces behind "yes and," what makes it useful, and why that's relevant to narrative gaming. Of course there's a wide gap between understanding those concepts and putting them into practice.

We focus on "making choices important" because it's a concrete goal for your contributions. "Tell a good story" or "have fun" are overarching hopes you might have for an RPG, but they can't help you in the middle of a game. They might even frustrate you by being elusive. "Yes and" helps you understand the structure of improvisation, but it's not a clear direction. As we've learned, it's also easy to misinterpret.

"Make choices important" is an immediate call to action that applies in almost every situation. Before we explain how to make choices important, let's take a quick look at exactly what some of those words mean in a storytelling context and what this goal is asking of us.

MAKE

This implies direct personal action. It's calling on *you* as a player to be a part of what makes the game interesting and fun. It lets you know that under this philosophy you have agency. Even if it's about collaboration, "make choices important" is something you have control over.

CHOICES

Using this word helps you make a vital assumption about the contributions of your fellow players. It implies that the ideas they bring to the table are intentional. It assumes they have introduced material to the text of the game because they find it interesting on some level. A lot of listening is unpacking what your collaborators care about and connecting it to what you care about. Treating all the ideas you are confronted with as choices sets you up to respect your collaborators and their ideas. That's a critical part of teamwork.

IMPORTANT

This is a versatile directive. There are all sorts of reasons something might be important to a story. An idea could make a situation really dramatic, it could make a particular image cool or exciting, or it could make a situation silly and fun to think about. In all those cases, important ideas drive us toward the little things that make playing fun. Your only responsibility is to examine what's out there and add significance to it. Sometimes that will fold into larger plot details that drive the game. Other times it will just make a given moment a little more interesting. It also asks you to invest in your collaboration. *Important* on some level means "relevant to you." If you're presented with an idea you don't find compelling, "make choices important" challenges you to add to it until you do.

HOW DO I DO IT?

With all that in mind, let's look at some techniques to use when looking to make choices important. Generally, we'll want to try three methods: *invest*, *connect*, and *elaborate*.

Investing is searching for something we find interesting about someone's idea. It's much easier to collaborate if you care about what's going on. Sometimes that happens organically, but other times it takes a little examination. All you need is something small to start with. Making something important to *you* will make it important to the game.

Connecting is linking ideas together. Relating what's happening now to what happened before—or what we *hope* will happen eventually—automatically makes ideas important. On a fundamental level, connecting ideas is how storytelling works. Every event, character, and image in your game carries a bit of significance. When those concepts connect it forms a story and their significance grows. It's also a great way to encourage collaboration. Connecting the ideas of several players helps them invest in each other passively.

Elaborating is putting your investment and connections into action by adding your own contribution. It also means making a contribution more important by simply expanding on what's already there.

The easiest way to put these concepts into action is by asking yourself questions about what's going on. Let's take a look at some potential questions:

INVEST
- What do I find cool about this?
- How could this situation make my character feel a strong emotion?
- What's the most interesting image this conjures in my mind?
- Why should we be excited about this?

CONNECT
- How does this relate to something that happened earlier?
- What implications does this have on my world?
- Is this related to another character in a way I have not considered?
- What here should be memorable later?

ELABORATE
- Can I raise the stakes?
- What do I think my fellow players want to see?
- Is there something related to what's happening that we haven't seen in the text?
- Can I complement this?

Now it's time to give it a try! Choose one of the following situations and ask one or two questions from the invest, connect, elaborate lists to make choices important:

Situation 1: *Charles rolled a successful strength check to open a locked door.*
Charles: *I got a 10. Eliana forces her way in.*

Situation 2: *A party of thieves is sorting out the loot from their last job and Tanya makes a request.*
Tanya: *Specs wants his share to be the paintings; my character is an art collector.*

Situation 3: *After a lucky roll, Puff the bard managed to score a crit against a stronger opponent.*
Blanca: *Go Puff! That's 17 damage after the crit!*

Situation 4: *Lee describes the appearance of an otherworldly monster.*
Lee (GM): *Pulling back the curtain you find the source of the music. The musicians move with an unnatural jerky quality. Their legs seem to dangle above the stage. When your eyes adjust to the light you can see large tentacles extending from their backs, moving these bodies like limp dolls. An indiscernible slithering mass behind them occasionally catches the light on damp slimy skin.*

For the purpose of this exercise, we can assume any history for the game these scenarios are attached to. What matters is understanding how these questions help us build.

Situation:

Method: Invest, Connect, Elaborate

Question:

Response:

You can respond to these scenarios in any number of ways as a GM or player. The same questions can produce different results, and it is even possible to combine multiple questions to produce a more elaborate response. If you're stuck, refer to the examples below for inspiration.

Situation 1: *Charles rolled a successful strength check to open a locked door.*
Charles: *I got a 10. Eliana forces her way in.*

Method: Invest, Connect, (Elaborate)

Question: Is there something related to what's happening that we haven't seen in the text?
We know Eliana used force to open the door, but Charles didn't identify what that looked like. We can make the choice to use force important by expanding the visual.

Response:

Eliana eyes the lock. Picking it will take time, and that's in short supply. She bends down to grab a loose brick from the alley. She weighs it in her hand, then slams it down on the door handle. The handle clatters to the ground alongside the brick as Eliana easily forces the damaged door open with a shoulder.

Now opening the door is a little more exciting, and Charles's decision to use force over guile is part of a critical assessment his character made.

Situation 2: *A party of thieves is sorting out the loot from their last job and Tanya makes a request.*

Tanya: *Specs wants his share to be the paintings; my character is an art collector.*

Method: Invest, (Connect,) Elaborate

Question: Is this related to another character in a way I have not considered? How does this relate to something that happened earlier?

Tanya made this request to incorporate the idea of Specs being an art collector into the narrative. Right now this is just an aesthetic choice. To make her choice important, we can use it as an opportunity to reveal new information.

Response:

Specs holds back a smirk. These paintings could sell for thousands more if brought to the right buyers. Buyers he happens to know. That smile quickly melts away as he looks over the last painting in the haul. The brush strokes give it away—it's a fake. Someone else must have got there first. After examining the frame he finds the insignia of your rivals, The Midnight Jacks.

Connecting Tanya's cosmetic choice to the next plot hook adds to both her character and the scene. First, Specs gets a cool moment as we implied he was using his specialized knowledge to get a bigger cut. That doesn't unbalance the party as the fake painting negates the extra money he would have received. It also makes the denouement more exciting by paving the way for the next adventure. All by using information we planned to reveal eventually anyway.

Situation 3: *After a lucky roll, Puff the bard managed to score a crit against a stronger opponent.*
Blanca: *Go Puff! That's 17 damage after the crit!*

Method: (Invest, Connect) Elaborate

Question: Is this related to another character in a way I have not considered? How could this situation make my character feel a strong emotion?
Most of our examples have been GMs reacting to PCs and PCs to GMs. It's also possible for a PC to react to another PC to make a choice or moment important.

Response:

Glorg watches Puff punch the necromancer. He flashes back to all of the moments he tried to instruct Puff in the ways of battle. He secretly feared the musician would never learn the war song. With this punch, he sees the potential he always believed was there come to life. Large tears well up in Glorg's eyes as he whispers—in the manner of a half-orc, which is a kind of low shout heard by everyone else—"Today Puff become a warrior. Today Puff am...a brother!" He charges into battle crying with joy.

Glorg's reaction makes Puff's crit an even bigger deal by deepening the relationship between the characters. It also continues to draw focus to the already exciting moment.

Situation 4: *Lee describes the appearance of an otherworldly monster.*

Lee (GM): *Pulling back the curtain you find the source of the music. The musicians move with an unnatural jerky quality. Their legs seem to dangle above the stage. When your eyes adjust to the light you can see large tentacles extending from their backs, moving these bodies like limp dolls. An indiscernible slithering mass behind them occasionally catches the light on damp slimy skin.*

Method: (Invest) Connect, Elaborate

Question: How could this situation make my character feel a strong emotion?

Here we're confronted with a monster. In many games a PC's first instinct is to fight. It's obvious that the GM put a lot of work into making that scene horrifying. Even if we dive into game mechanics, we can reward that effort and make the description important by having characters react emotionally. Fear is on the table, and we can play it up even if our characters do something brave.

Response:

Sam feels dizzy as sweat gathers on his brow. He's stopped breathing. When he finally lets his breath out, it's in a scream no one can hear. It's drowned out by the sound of his tommy gun. He doesn't even remember pulling the trigger.

Our hard-boiled mobster Sam stayed true to himself and lashed out violently, but we paid homage to the terror of the GM's monster.

CREATING AGREEMENT

Everyone agreeing on what's important is an ideal situation. That's not always immediately possible. Sometimes players want different things. When disagreements pop up, it can be difficult to see how to move forward, especially if you're prioritizing collaboration. In these circumstances, "make choices important" might seem like an unattainable goal, or at least one that won't help you get back on track.

Let's say you're running a superhero game. You want to run a session or two where the PCs team up with a supervillain. Some players might jump at the chance to forgive and reform a criminal. There is a chance that a few will simply not be able to justify their character working with a villain, which puts a block on the story.

Often when a player wants their character to walk away from a planned adventure, it's not because they don't want to play; it's because they can't connect the scenario to what they see as defining character traits. If they go along, they'll be sacrificing authenticity, and for so many players, authenticity is the point.

A player whose character refuses to work with a villain is expressing something important about their character that needs to be recognized in order for the story to move forward. In this case, they have a moral code that needs to be satisfied or highlighted. Just going along with the villain because that's what the plot demands doesn't cut it.

In these situations you need to:

1. **Understand what's important.** If something is important enough to prevent a player from participating alongside the group, then you need to know what it is. An open meta discussion is usually the easiest way to identify what matters. The player is not their character. They understand things the character does not. If you understand what is important to the player, you'll know what needs to be prioritized in crafting a solution.
2. **Acknowledge its importance.** Especially when you're frustrated, it's tempting to downplay the importance of obstacles. That's actually counterproductive here! A player who feels heard and understood will be more ready to find a solution. People are

more important than games. Even if the current plot would be easier if the player thought differently, their feelings matter more. It's easier to change a story than a person. Validation is the best foundation for collaboration.

3. **State your needs.** You are also part of this! Your needs are as important as the other players'. Be frank about what it will take to keep the game moving. It's okay to be upfront and identify specifically what diminishes your experience and what is most essential to you.

4. **Ask what needs to change.** After identifying what's important to every player involved in the disagreement, it's a simple matter of connecting those ideas in the fiction. Usually this means changing the context of what's going on or agreeing to focus on a new idea within the original scenario.

5. **Make changes and move forward.** Apply any discussed changes to the fiction to make sure the new framing fits.

Let's apply this method to our superhero game:

Clarissa: *"I'll never trust you, after what you did to Alpha Jock. If you're working with him I'm off the team."*

Juanita (GM): *I want to take a quick pause. Clarissa, it makes sense that Scream Queen doesn't want to willingly work with The Slasher.*

Clarissa: *Yeah, there is too much history there.*

Juanita (GM): *A lot of what I prepared depends on the team being with The Slasher. Is there a way you could have fun going with the group and hating his guts the whole time? Or is this just something you're not comfortable with?*

Clarissa: *I don't think it's a personal comfort issue. I'm just trying to picture it and it doesn't make sense for the character.*

Juanita (GM): *What would make this mission so important that Scream Queen couldn't walk away?*

Clarissa: *Well, she definitely wants The Slasher put away. She can't forgive him and it's asking a lot to have her work closely with him.*

Juanita (GM): *I think I got it: "I thought you might feel that way, Scream Queen. That's why once we've stopped The Deadly Twist, I am willing to surrender my cursed knife. Without it, I have no power. I'll be vulnerable to mundane punishments. I'd never be able to harm anyone again."*

Clarissa: *"Like I'd believe that. What are you planning?"*

Juanita (GM): *"I'm quite serious, Scream Queen. I'll be working with your friends whether you trust me or not. However, I'll only surrender the knife to you."*

Clarissa: *"Fine." I can't wait to bust this creep.*

In order to satisfy Scream Queen's history and moral code, Clarissa needed the opportunity to bring justice to The Slasher. With that in place, Juanita was able to pursue her scenario mostly unchanged. They'll still need to address the new plot hook, but Juanita will have the opportunity to prepare for that after they play through what she has prepared.

BEHIND A SCREEN

Solving a problem like this doesn't *need* to happen during gameplay. In fact sometimes taking a moment to step away from the group and discuss things privately makes it easier. Remember, expressing both concern and enthusiasm are acts of vulnerability. The whole group needs to understand any changes you decide on, so feel free to take preliminary steps in private and hash out final steps with the rest of the group.

This reveals a key concept that allows "make choices important" to function. When you "make choices important" you actually make *people* important. On the surface, you are validating ideas to move the story. However, when you do that, you're actually validating your fellow players. It feels good to have someone listen to you, and to see your ideas flourish. That's part of what makes RPGs fun!

"Make choices important" will help you build strong fiction. Making people important will help you keep your group together while doing that.

Pacing

Have you ever walked away from a video game or movie because it was repetitive, confusing, or boring? Most of those problems are driven by poor *pacing*. A story can have individual elements that you find exciting like explosions, kissing, or stunts but still fall flat if those elements aren't presented well. RPGs work the same way. It's not just what you include in your narrative that makes it great, but how you pace it. The audience structure for RPGs makes pacing a challenge. At times you are dedicating moments to individual audience members. A major story beat for one character doesn't necessarily translate to excitement for everyone at the table.

This chapter will teach you how to create variation between events in a game, explain the basics of story beats, and show you how to direct the spotlight on PCs as characters and players.

Changing Scale versus Changing Type

Story beats are how we chart the overall plot of a narrative. They can be specific events in scenes or the scenes themselves. Part of pacing is making story beats feel distinct from one another. This helps you cultivate audience interest. If every scene in your game is a combat scene, it will start to wear on players, even if everyone really likes combat.

One way to fix this pacing issue is to change the *scale* of an encounter. A change in scale works by manipulating the audience's perception of stakes. If your party fights a wolf in their first scene, you can make the next scene distinct simply by adding more wolves. *Anything* you do to alter the audience's perception of a threat changes the scale. Instead of confronting your party with three normal wolves, for example, you can challenge them with a single giant superwolf.

A change in scale generally follows the flow of the plot. As the game moves forward, the scale of the threats increases. This creates a sense of progression; you started with an easy fight, and now the stakes are higher because you're facing more or larger opponents.

There are diminishing returns on changes in scale. The difference between fighting one wolf and fighting three wolves is pretty significant, but the difference between ten and twelve has less impact.

You can maintain an interesting pace by introducing a change in *type*. Rather than following your three-wolf combat with yet another fight against wolves, you could add a scene about tracking the superwolf. A tracking scene won't have the same life-and-death stakes as your combats, and that's actually a good thing! If death is always on the table, it doesn't have the same impact. Tracking the superwolf will also give your party time to think about why the upcoming encounter will be different.

That's the value of a change in type: it makes the story feel dynamic without constantly raising the stakes or altering the power of the PCs.

DEVELOPMENT CYCLES

RPGs pioneered many fundamental concepts that appear as staples of modern video games; these include hit points, experience, and character levels. That influence goes both ways, as video games are the origin of many RPG conventions. This section about changes in "scale" and "type" is adapted from a lecture by Extra Credits analyzing differences in "scale" and "kind" in video games.

Upbeat and Downbeat

A general progression in story beats is good, but always ramping up makes it difficult to introduce your next move. A change in type also relates to reward and satisfaction PCs feel after a given scene.

Feelings of accomplishment and release of tension create an **upbeat**, while feelings of struggle or mounting tension create a **downbeat**.

If the party barely crawls away from their wolf fight, gets chewed out by their employers over their belief in the existence of wolf cults, and then has another difficult battle with the superwolf, the game will feel like a slog. It's a progression, but a progression of downbeats. Repeated challenges with little to no reward.

Even a slight change will make a huge difference. If the events leading to the superwolf fight include surviving a wolf encounter and successfully battling wolf cults, the challenges will feel more varied and manageable.

Tension is the most important aspect of evaluating your upbeats and downbeats. You want tension to ebb and flow through a game to make it feel dynamic. Generally, tension mounts as you approach a climax of a session or story arc, but it can rise and fall throughout to create change in type.

Upbeats and downbeats are more complex in RPGs because *spotlight* (which we'll address shortly) factors into how moments are perceived by your audience. In most stories we look at story beats through the lens of protagonists and story movement. However, a character downbeat in an RPG can also be an upbeat for the player because they have the spotlight.

Six Basic Scene Types

To help you understand how to create a change in type, we'll explain six major scene types common to RPGs—action, discovery, interpersonal, emotional, challenge, and preparation. These are broad categories that can be broken down further to create more granular distinction, but for our purposes, we're going to focus on the big picture.

It's also possible for a given scene to comfortably fit more than one category. Mixing and matching scene types will help you cover more storytelling ground faster. You need to understand them individually first so you can use them together more effectively.

ACTION

An *action* scene is any scene driven by physical events. Combat, chases, and overcoming physical obstacles all fall under the umbrella of action.

During action scenes the stakes are high and PCs make explosive choices. Action is typically tied to a climax, because it simplifies complex stakes as it raises them. A character living, dying, or hurt is pretty much as intense as stakes can get. Action is almost always an upbeat, providing a release in tension.

You can use action scenes to build tension depending on how you position the stakes and rewards. For example, you can use a difficult fight to establish a threat or a chase to make danger explicit. Players will still need a downbeat to process increased tension from action scenes.

Action scenes have a complex relationship with pacing in RPGs. Most traditional systems use what's called an **initiative**, where players take turns describing short moments in great detail. An action scene lasting a few seconds in fiction can take over an hour to play out at the table. Despite having upbeat energy, action in initiative can feel slow. It's important to remember that as you consider how action scenes affect your pace. High-intensity events can sometimes really drag.

DISCOVERY

A *discovery* scene revolves around revealing information to the audience or PCs. Activities like investigation, research, or interrogation are discovery scenes. Discovery builds tension in most circumstances, providing protagonists with information they need to take action.

Discovery is typically a downbeat because events usually unfold over long periods of time and information raises more questions than it answers. In mystery or horror games discovery scenes slowly bring the overarching mystery or the horrible monster into focus.

You can use a discovery to release tension by answering a central question—"you've been betrayed," "the butler did it," "there is more than one monster"—but major revelations typically still precede action scenes where protagonists act on what they learn to release tension.

Skill-driven RPGs make discovery scenes an unevenly distributed spotlight upbeat. Not every PC will have tools to interact with a discovery scene. Some characters will take the spotlight while others take a downbeat. Paying attention to whose strengths are being featured will help you determine how this type of scene is impacting the pace of your narrative for individual players.

INTERPERSONAL

Role-play is the defining trait of *interpersonal* scenes. Any scene driven by dialogue from intimate heart-to-heart chats to tense negotiations is interpersonal. This counts for intra-party PC-to-PC conversations and conversations with NPCs. As far as tension goes, interpersonal scenes are fairly versatile. Getting information from a contact might build tension, and an explosive argument might release tension.

Interpersonal scenes make excellent downbeats. They're some of the strongest moments tied to character, which makes them a catalyst for tying the PCs to the plot. Interpersonal scenes allow players to process the events of the game and develop their characters naturally in fiction.

This scene type frequently mixes with the other types. It's not unusual to have characters talk for the sake of talking, but typically conversations are accompanied by discovery, emotional exploration, or even action.

EMOTIONAL

These scenes are driven by *emotional* exploration for major characters. They deepen an intimate connection between the audience and PCs. For narrative play they are essential, but only some role-playing systems provide mechanical support for emotional scenes.

Emotional scenes usually appear as a component or accessory to another scene. It's possible to create purely emotional scenes through dialogue-free flashbacks, vignettes, or even out-of-character exposition. Still, emotional exploration can be used as a kind of seasoning to enhance tension in action, discovery, and interpersonal scenes.

Purely emotional scenes are typically downbeats that have a tight focus on individual PCs. If you're doing a vignette, it's probably to give a character the opportunity to emote. Introducing emotional undertones to another scene almost always builds tension.

CHALLENGE

One of the most frequently used scene types is *challenge*. Riddles, puzzles, and strategic action create challenge scenes. They incorporate a challenge external to the fiction into the game, directly engaging the players alongside their characters. Some RPGs incorporate challenge through resource management and tactical miniature systems. Others put logic puzzles or riddles into adventures.

From a narrative perspective, challenge scenes don't do much to directly influence the plot as an upbeat or downbeat. However, they provide a valuable opportunity to give the game a refreshing change in type, and foster a feeling of **immersion**. When you present a player with a riddle or puzzle they solve it the same way their character does. That connection can open up players to engage with other aspects of the game with greater depth.

PREPARATION

The final major scene type is fairly unique to RPGs. *Preparation* scenes focus on the character's readying themselves for the next stages in the plot. Activities like mechanical maintenance, shopping, and in-character planning define preparation scenes.

Preparation is not the sort of thing you'd expect to drive the narrative in other mediums. We sometimes get to see characters concoct a plan in novels, films, and TV, but usually it's a tool to set expectations. In RPGs preparation is a core aspect of gameplay. Making decisions on a character's behalf is part of the fun of role-playing. It also gives players an opportunity to indulge the power fantasy aspects of role-playing.

These scenes are almost exclusively downbeats. Preparation is a great opportunity to give a party a chance to breathe. It allows players to absorb the events of the game thus far before diving back into chaos. It also helps GMs understand a party's expectations for future scenes so they can more effectively meet or subvert them.

Spotlight

Now that we understand the basics of pacing, it's time for the audience to make things complicated. As we pointed out in our explanation of upbeats and downbeats, not every scene serves your entire audience in the same way.

Most fiction is passive—the audience just has to absorb the story. In RPGs the audience actively generates the story, so you have to consider how people are being engaged as participants as part of your pacing. A game can have a series of exciting scenes full of emotional and plot development. However, if these scenes exclude even one PC, the narrative is failing one of the players.

If a character is in the spotlight they are actively participating in a scene. This can be through game mechanics, role-play, or general collaboration. It's tricky to juggle so many character stories with only a few hours in each session. It's natural for a given gaming session to spotlight one or two PCs more than others. However, it's important to ensure no one gets left too far behind.

As a rule, we recommend giving each player one significant event every session. To help you do that, let's look at the different ways to create spotlight and how they impact the audience experience.

COLLECTIVE SPOTLIGHT

Some events involve everyone. We call these *collective spotlight* scenes. Usually, games provide mechanical support to make these scenes easier to facilitate.

The easiest example of this type of scene is combat in a traditional RPG. Every player gets a turn, and everyone's character has relevant abilities. Not every character is built the same way. There are definitely some characters that shine more than others, but everyone is sharing the stage.

Players should feel some level of personal audience satisfaction from a collective scene, but it probably won't define the session for most players. In some ways, participation in a collective scene is the bare minimum for players. After all, "you're going to matter in this story" is part of the basic social contract for RPGs.

Despite the lower intensity of audience engagement, collective scenes are critical to a game's narrative structure. Collective events essentialize the RPG experience of everyone working together. It's a good idea to build your climaxes around collective scenes. If everyone is present and active during major narrative events, then the plot feels like it's under joint ownership.

DON'T SPLIT THE PARTY!

Age-old RPG advice instructs GMs and players to keep PCs together. Most games assume PCs are acting as a unit, so PCs are mechanically incentivized to work that way. It also makes the plot more manageable because the GM doesn't have to hop back and forth between scenes. Every time a PC is not on screen, the game is creating downtime for someone.

COMPETENCE SPOTLIGHT

A *competence spotlight* is personalized and an easy way to create a spotlight upbeat. Competence spotlights are moments that directly engage the strengths/preferences of a PC or the player. We say "moment" rather than "scene" because a competence spotlight can be a component of a larger scene. These moments indulge the power fantasy potential of RPGs and create a sense of accomplishment.

A competence spotlight can engage players through their character, or directly as individuals. Giving a PC a competence spotlight means creating the opportunity to do what they do best. You can break down this type of competence into three categories: mechanical, experiential, and personality.

- **Mechanical** is competence provided by the rules of the game, like a challenge a character is suited to overcome based on their stats.
- **Experiential** competence is based on the character's history or any kind of knowledge the player has full agency over.
- **Personality** spotlights allow a character to behave in a way that feels iconically *them*.

Here are some examples of competence spotlights as they apply to different characters:

Spit is an elderly pirate with a crass sense of humor. He's older than everyone else on the ship, but that means he knows things:

- **Mechanical:** A knowledge roll about the customs of a particular port.
- **Experiential:** An opportunity to tell the story of an old pirate legend.
- **Personality:** The chance to make an innuendo.

Ashley Blazebuck is a teenager and lead singer for her glam punk band with a grudge against the world. She likes getting in fights more than she likes expressing her emotions:

- **Mechanical:** A singing competition where she really gets to wail.
- **Experiential:** A chance to talk about her favorite bands.
- **Personality:** An opportunity to overtly deny her crush on her classmate and stage manager, Randy Buckthorn.

Inspector Jackie is a straitlaced Hong Kong detective who always seems to get in over his head:

- **Mechanical:** The opportunity to resolve a dangerous situation using martial arts.
- **Experiential:** A chance to be familiar with an NPC based on his adventures in the past.

- **Personality:** The opportunity to resolve a dangerous situation using martial arts, while carefully balancing a tray of priceless porcelain statues he does not want to damage.

You can also create a competence spotlight for a player by giving them an opportunity to incorporate one of their real-life talents into the game. Your friends probably don't have character sheets with all of their skills listed, but if you know something about them, you can give them an opportunity to show off. Focusing on player competence helps you frame scenes to resolve in more satisfying ways. You can even use this spotlight to work a player into a scene where their character isn't present. Here are examples of player competence spotlights:

- A scene that calls on an actor to play out a dramatic conversation.
- A battle that calls on a strategically minded player to concoct a cunning plan.
- Asking a historian to use their experience to help shape the setting.
- Checking in with an experienced player about a rule.
- Referencing a story the player is deeply familiar with.

A spotlight on player competence isn't as valuable as spotlighting their character, but it still makes the narrative more personal.

ROLE-PLAY SPOTLIGHT

When a character is on screen in a film, the narrative is highlighting their importance. The protagonist's experience of events is as important as the plot itself. Giving players the opportunity to portray their characters and investigate their relationship to the story is an essential part of RPGs. The most obvious way to engage this spotlight is dialogue. When a player has an opportunity to speak in character, they can put personality into the plot. It fosters an emotional connection between player and PC. Giving voice to a character makes any movement in the plot more meaningful.

Role-play spotlights aren't just about acting; they're about portrayal—representing the character in the narrative. Portrayal can manifest in how a character is described. Any time the text is focused on a character, you create a role-play spotlight.

These scenes tend to serve a small number of players better. You can get a lot of mileage out of two or three PCs interacting. The more a game can focus on a single character, the more effective it will be as a role-play spotlight.

PLOT SPOTLIGHT

The plot of a game is shared among all of the players. As the story unfolds, there will be some events that are more relevant to individual characters than they are to the group. *Plot spotlights* make game events directly relevant to a PC's personal narrative.

Sometimes plot spotlights drive a session; for example, imagine a bounty hunter chasing a PC for crimes committed in their backstory. An event like that is likely to put the PC in question at the center of the story. A plot spotlight can also have a relatively small impact on ongoing events, like seeing the crest of the assassin school that one of the PCs escaped from. It's significant to the PC in question, but it won't define the session.

MECHANICAL FAILURE

Some RPGs have negative traits as part of character creation. A player can give their character mechanical and narrative disadvantages in exchange for resources. Many negative narrative traits like "nemesis," "evil twin," or "enemy to [group]" *do* place narrative obstacles in a PC's way, but they also provide opportunities for spotlight. Having multiple plot hooks as negative traits can actually favor that player's experience. Consider that when deciding which traits to include in your game.

It's possible for events surrounding a plot spotlight to engage the entire party. For example, suppose a team of teen superheroes is battling with one member's villainous parent. Everyone will be involved in the fight, but it's more directly relevant to the character fighting their family. It's important to note other players might feel as though their characters are out of focus, even if they are participating normally.

Plot spotlights honor PC backstories. They're a guaranteed way to make someone's choices important.

Giving and Taking Focus

The GM has a tremendous amount of influence over a game's pace. However, when it comes to spotlight, every player at the table has some ability to influence the experience of other players. PCs choose how their characters react to events, but those choices affect the flow of the narrative. It's possible to choose actions that take the spotlight or pass it on to other players.

In improv we call the act of moving attention around in a scene *giving and taking focus*. Certain choices move you into the spotlight and pull focus toward you, while others create space for your collaborators to take the spotlight.

WHAT TAKES FOCUS AND WHAT GIVES FOCUS?

Any time a player frames a scene around their actions, or the results of a PC's actions affect primarily themselves, they are taking focus. Taking focus isn't a bad thing. Sometimes you need to take decisive action when the plot, the GM, or the narrative convention calls for a character to step into the spotlight and fulfill their role. If nobody ever took focus, nothing would happen. Giving focus occurs when you act to set up success for another PC, add value to another PC's idea, or generally draw attention to something outside of yourself. Giving focus is part of active collaboration.

Taking Focus	Giving Focus
I spray the tentacles with bullets hoping to kill the beast.	I shoot the tentacles to draw the beast's attention while everyone completes the ritual.
"We're gonna melt you, ya undead nerd."	"I have seen Glorg here break more bones than I can count, and you're *made* of bones, sooooo..."
I use a net arrow to try to make the person falling stick safely to the wall of the building.	I fire an arrow into the wall so Springheel Jack can jump off it to catch the falling civilian.
I pocket one of the bills lying on the ground while no one is looking.	I pocket one of the bills lying on the ground before making eye contact with Sonja. Then I carefully try to place it where it was before.

It's not traditionally a PC responsibility to watch the spotlight on behalf of one another, but putting the goal of everyone having fun over personal satisfaction opens up new narrative possibilities. It also makes the work of tracking who is getting the spotlight easier for the GM to manage.

Engagement

By now we understand the power words have to influence a game. However, words are only a part of your instrument. RPGs are immersive and players interact with the game on multiple levels. *How* you present text—through speech, writing, props, or other means—also has a tremendous impact on an audience's experience of the story. How players react to their collaborators has an impact as well. There are innumerable things you can do to add to your game's story: creating handouts and props, delivering your dialogue with passion and skill, scoring sessions with background music, and just actively responding to events at the table to name a few. All of this falls under the umbrella of engagement or buy-in.

Obviously we can't explore everything you can possibly do to contribute to a game. Instead, this chapter will help you understand how engagement functions and give you some ways to foster it at your table.

Vulnerability and Enthusiasm

Role-playing is an intimate art form. Players sink into the headspace of characters and do creative work together in real time. Think of how often people ask others to wait until something is finished before they decide it's okay to share. It's a big deal to invite someone into your creative space and exchange ideas.

It's common to think of vulnerability as exposing flaws or weaknesses. However, it's also a vulnerable act to express interest or enthusiasm. Even saying "I think this is cool" lets people into your head. Storytelling is an act of creative expression; it tells people something about who you are. The more comfortable you get with sharing yourself, the more unique your storytelling will be. It also increases the likelihood that you'll enjoy yourself more because the game will be a better reflection of what you like.

There's a double-edged sword here. If vulnerability is met with rejection, it can really take someone out of a game or hurt them personally. Narrative gameplay challenges you to share more of yourself because it's part of the artistic process. In doing that, players open up to real emotional investment. This isn't something to be afraid of, but it is something to be cautious about.

DAMAGE AND BLEED

Emotional investment sometimes opens up players to experiencing the emotions their characters feel. It's also possible for players to take their real-life emotions and put them into the game. This process has been named *bleed* by game designer and scholar Emily Care Boss, because emotions from one environment bleed into another.

Bleed isn't inherently bad but it does carry risk. Negative emotions can spill over from one place to another, potentially hurting the game and the people playing.

Bleed can also be affirming or therapeutic. The ability to experience or examine emotions from a different point of view is invaluable to some. Regardless of the effects it's important to check in with yourself and your friends to be aware of emotions resulting from bleed, so they don't turn into problems.

Vulnerability helps make a game more interesting, and enthusiasm keeps that experience positive. Enthusiasm is an energy you put into what you do when you play. When you're enthusiastic, you're actively showing that you're enjoying the game. That makes the people you're playing with feel good about their ideas, freeing them to be vulnerable.

Just one enthusiastic player can lead a whole table to engage on a new level. Understanding that these concepts are at the core of engagement should help you build your own tools to engage your table.

Engage!

Now that we know what we're aiming for, let's take a look at different approaches to cultivating engagement. We'll simplify larger concepts into easy-to-try techniques. Many of these work for PCs and GMs alike.

MIN-MAXING

Some players try to build more effective characters by "min-maxing," putting their resources into specific abilities to make them as effective as possible, while minimizing their investment in unrelated abilities. This logic can be applied to your playing experience too! Any of the ideas presented here can enhance a game, but they might not be a perfect match for each player, or each group. It says nothing about your skill as a player if you don't find these techniques helpful. It's always great to try something new, but it's only worth keeping around if you think it's fun.

VOICES

When you're in an RPG, speaking in character gives you an opportunity to actually deliver lines the way actors do in plays. Creating a distinction between your voice and a character's voice can add depth to a game.

First, it provides a clear separation between out-of-character and in-character speech. That makes it easier for other players to engage with the character by signaling when that character is present. This goes hand-in-hand with the idea of immersion. A dialogue between two characters with special voices is, in a way, a real-world manifestation of the events of your game. The conversation at the table is the same as the conversation in the game world.

A change in voice also allows some players to connect with their characters on a deeper level. One of the performance techniques in improv is "changing your spine," where a performer adopts a new posture in order to portray a character. The theory is that each person has a default posture and mannerisms that accompany their personality. Adopting a new posture, or changing your spine, creates a ripple effect on other behavioral attributes that make up a character.

Changing your voice operates on the same principle. Speaking like a sly con artist makes it feel more natural to say things you'd never say in your everyday life. A new voice can help you make discoveries about a character's personality.

Finally, character voices also inject energy into a game. People tend to be more animated in character, which sets a more enthusiastic tone. Sitting at a table and talking to friends is something we do in everyday life. The sort of interaction you have playing an RPG is special. Silly voices help create a separation between hanging out and playing the game.

If you want to develop and practice new voices, head to Chapter 15 for an exercise!

UP YOUR ACTING GAME

Character voices are the tip of the iceberg for performance skills. Manipulating your cadence and tone during narration can have a huge impact on your text. It makes a big difference whether you use a playful smile or a dramatic whisper when describing the movement of a shadow.

Physically emoting also contributes to the experience of a game. Humans react to emotional displays through a natural and subconscious process. That's part of what makes acting a compelling art form! Incorporating a physical performance into your character portrayal and narration will add a new dimension to your experience.

LOREKEEPING

One piece of advice that you'll see pretty often in role-playing circles is "be a fan of your characters." This generally means if you play with characters that interest you, you'll be more excited to tell stories about them. Depending on how you engage with fandom, this concept could open you up to seeing your games in a new way.

Being part of the audience means you get to indulge your inner fan when you play. Think of how you engage with your favorite TV shows, comics, and movies. Do you draw fan art? Keep track of events and continuity? Maybe write a little fan fiction? All of that can become a part of the table through a *lore site*.

WHAT THE HECK IS A LORE SITE?

A lore site is an online encyclopedia for your game world. Just like real-world reference sites and fan-made information catalogs, lore sites track known information about your campaign. Characters, locations, objects, and events can be recorded and tracked by any of the players.

There are plenty of free resources for making an online encyclopedia and even a few purpose-built game-tracking tools.

A site for your campaign can be a collaborative effort that provides a very practical advantage for story-based play. For GMs, a database of characters, locations, and events makes juggling all of the important plot threads a little easier. If the PCs contribute, it can highlight what players connect with most. PCs don't always have the benefit of seeing the story laid out for them. It's natural to focus on your character during a game, but that can make you miss a lot. Chronicling the game can provide the motivation to take more in. It also adds a resource for players who have trouble retaining all the details.

Lore sites provide a platform for people to bring more of their creative talents into a game outside regular gaming sessions. Drawing a battle scene while it's unfolding at the table can pull your attention away from the action. However, uploading a sketch you do between sessions to a shared lore site adds to everyone's experience. Some creative tasks take a little privacy and focus to execute. Maintaining a place to share also gives new purpose to that kind of creativity.

When you treat your own work with the same kind of enthusiasm you have for other stories you love, it adds a new dimension to your creativity. A site is just one way to turn that sort of engagement into a group activity.

BONUS XP

The idea behind lorekeeping is to add another dimension to your game by making it easier to understand, and creating the feel of a group project. Streaming or recording sessions as actual play also creates a record of game information and treats playing like a production. Even if the recordings are just for you and your friends, the process makes playing feel more important.

Fan art, fan fiction, and so many other fandom-related activities give you the opportunity to revisit and appreciate your own work. That can help you grow creatively and feel good about what you're doing!

SIDE STORIES

Not everything needs to happen strictly at the table. For so many people, playing just a few times a month isn't enough. Especially if RPGs are your primary creative outlet! **Personal play** is the process of indulging in game-related creativity between actual sessions.

GMs have lots of personal play activities built into their role. Creating adventures, encounters, and game accessories all fall under the umbrella of personal play. For some GMs, the work associated with game preparation is its own rewarding hobby. People even write settings and scenarios for games they aren't actively running.

YOU MIGHT BE A GAME DESIGNER!

Some people treat the "game designer" title as something that comes with creating published work or having professional status. However, one of the essential functions of GMing is an act of game design! Choosing which rules apply to which situations is an active application of the theory designers use when they write rules.

If you create your own settings, campaigns, and adventures, you're doing the work of a designer. The only difference between most GMs and folks we think of as game designers is how they share their work.

PCs, on the other hand, don't have access to much extracurricular activity playing with a traditional approach. After creating a character and backstory, there's not much for PCs to do between sessions.

That's why we recommend taking time to create *side stories*. Side stories are narrative events that don't require developing the central plot. They allow players to explore characters and their relationships in a pressure-free environment. Think of side stories as like "bottle episodes" on TV; they put characters in situations where most of the action revolves around social interaction.

A side story can focus on your PC and someone else from the party. It can also focus on that character's past or explore the personality of an NPC. The events of side stories can be purely hypothetical or even put characters in different universes. You'd be surprised how easy it is to separate a character from their environment and still make interesting discoveries. It's a perfect space in which to refine ideas that come from vulnerable places before bringing them to the group.

You can write or think through a side scene alone. This might feel weird, as a PC typically only speaks for their own character. However, understanding how other characters think and act will help you play to their strengths more when you *do* get to play. Playing by post through a forum, chat service, email, or in person, PCs can enjoy side stories together.

If you're looking for some structure for creating side stories for personal play, check out the side scene exercises in Chapter 23!

PART 2

Advanced Playing Techniques

You will have an easier time learning the lessons in this section if you abandon preconceived notions of what art is supposed to be.

Some people grapple with the idea of treating their own work as art because we're instructed on a cultural level to believe if something is art, it's necessarily inaccessible. Some people assert there are institutional hurdles you need to overcome in order to make art. A story needs to be written and published, music needs to be performed for an audience, a painting needs to be in a gallery.

Hierarchies and barriers surrounding artistic expression impede people's ability to value creative efforts they enjoy. There are folks who insist that things like animation, comics, and games are not the right sort of entertainment to carry artistic worth. This needlessly limits the creative potential of rich, expressive mediums. Even if we don't harbor these toxic beliefs about the art we love, it's still possible for hierarchies to harm us by separating our own creative work from the work that inspires us.

It is not pretentious to acknowledge that your games are a form of art. Art is fluid and can appear as an incidental part of many activities. RPGs blend storytelling and performance, which we recognize as artistic pursuits away from the table. Even if you don't intend to play your game as a form of artistic expression, even if you just want to have fun, those artistic pursuits are still a part of what you do when you play.

It will be much easier to learn the techniques in this section if you accept that everything that happens at your table possesses some kind of artistic value. Treating games as part of the language of artistic expression will help you grow to express yourself with greater confidence. Being able to evaluate your play the way you would a novel or film will help you take advantage of artistic techniques pioneered in literature and movies. It will also allow you to treat the creativity possessed by you and your friends with the respect it deserves.

Introduction to GMing Style and Making Choices with Intention

It's both a blessing and a curse that there is so much advice about how to be a good GM. So much goes into running a game—there's no limit to the ways you can hone your craft. Every year there are countless words written in books, on blogs, and in forums with advice about ways to do it. Unfortunately, some of this advice suggests some approaches are inherently better than others. Encountering advice that suggests your preferred approach isn't any good makes the learning process demoralizing.

Applying this logic to other art forms reveals how flawed it is. Is painting with oil superior to acrylics? Is sculpture more artistically valuable than architecture? Does banjo music have more merit than guitar? How could those claims possibly be evaluated? On whose authority do we accept that judgment?

It's always good to study and grow, but you're not really looking to be a better GM. You're looking to develop your personal style. Some advice will be more relevant to that goal than the rest. In this chapter, we'll provide an overview of some basic stylistic divisions. Hopefully, that will help you define what skills you want to develop. We'll also give you the basic secret to making your style matter.

Improvisation and Preparation

On some level all role-playing is improvisational. The game revolves around players making stuff up in the moment. When we reference a GM who prefers an "improvisational" style, we mean someone who prefers to just sit down and play.

An improvisational approach tends to work best with games that are light on mechanics. Having a flexible system will help you avoid getting bogged down in details. It's much easier to introduce new ideas on the spot if you don't have to spend time establishing stats for them.

It *is* possible to improvise with mechanically robust games. In those cases, you should have a greater familiarity with the game. Just be aware: the more complex a game, the greater its potential to fall apart when you start making changes and omitting details.

Unsurprisingly, an improvisational style depends heavily on being comfortable with not having all the answers and having a strong foundation of collaborative skills. No one has good ideas all the time. Working with a group reduces the creative pressure on you and it's great for your group. As we pointed out in Chapter 6, good improvisation is built on active listening.

Being an improvisational GM doesn't mean you have to do *everything* yourself. There are plenty of gaming accessories you can use to make your job easier. For example, you don't have to do detailed world building if you set your game in an established universe. Setting a game in the real world or the world of your favorite novel, comic, film, or TV franchise answers a ton of questions, giving you the freedom to focus your creativity on the PCs. Working with a familiar setting also empowers your players to make assumptions, which aids collaboration.

Game aids like setting books, bestiaries, and prepublished adventures are purpose-built to provide GMs with a strong framework to build on. You don't have to worry about creating balanced combats or working up statistics for NPCs if you use something created by a professional designer. Using pregenerated material doesn't mean you're beholden to following someone else's script either. As the GM you get to decide what you want to use. A detailed NPC from a published adventure might just be a convenient collection of level-appropriate combat information for your otherwise original adventure.

PREPARATION

Most folks think of RPGs as being experienced solely at the table, that the only time you actually play the game is when you're actively role-playing with other people. The idea of play often extends much further than what happens in a session though; creativity can happen well before people actually start rolling dice.

A preparation-based GM takes time to flesh out details before PCs get involved—for example, taking the time to determine how an intelligence organization is structured or what a spy's specific mission is before running an espionage game. If players want to interrogate a captured NPC, knowing the mission will tell the GM what information the NPC is trying to protect. Understanding the organization's structure will tell the GM what information the NPC might have access to. Spending time with story prep like this can help a game world feel consistent and nuanced.

NONBINARY GAMING IDENTITY

The divide between improvisation and preparation is not a hard line but a spectrum. A GM can invest preparation in some areas and leave others to be sorted out in the moment. It's really unlikely that someone will keep to one approach over the other all the time.

That's true for the other styles in this chapter too! Adopting one of these styles doesn't mean a commitment to the core philosophy; it just means you're choosing a particular technique. Being consistent isn't as important as understanding how each approach affects your experience.

Preparation also opens up GMs to a certain level of production value for their games. Taking time to create accessories like handouts, props, or miniatures, or even preparing soundtracks can enhance a game by making it feel more immersive.

Living World versus Living Narrative

One of the major GM responsibilities is controlling the game world. How you approach that responsibility creates another stylistic divide: between *living world* and *living narrative*.

LIVING WORLD

A living world style treats the game world as a "real" place, of which the players see only a part. Every PC choice has the potential to create a storytelling domino effect that ripples through the game world.

If a group of monster hunter PCs in an urban fantasy game take down a gang of arms-dealing werewolves, what happens? Immediately, the monster hunting PCs have shut down the werewolf criminal enterprise. However, if the setting is a living world, it could mean one of the other factions in your setting now have an opportunity to expand their operation into vacant werewolf territory. With the werewolves out of the way, it's time for vampire racketeers to fill the vacancy.

A GM presiding over a living world sometimes keeps track of information the PCs don't have access to. Even if the PCs didn't know about or pay attention to the vampire racketeers, they exist and act with their own agency. The goal is to create the feeling of a real world full of unintended consequences. Not everything in a living world needs to directly impact the PCs, but it exists if they choose to seek it out.

LIVING NARRATIVE

With this approach, characters, locations, and events exist only to serve the PC's story. The GM doesn't bother to chart "off screen" events until the PCs seek information or there is a need generated by the narrative.

Returning to the urban fantasy example, the only NPCs the GM is concerned with are the werewolves. As long as the PCs are focused on them, the werewolves are actively reacting. Once they've been defeated, the werewolves disappear. The vampires are created once the PCs need a new antagonist to drive their actions. Instead of maintaining a web of interconnected factions to bring in as necessary, a living narrative assumes such factions *must* exist and generates them as needed.

With a living narrative, the reality of the game is dictated by player whims and narrative structures. Since nothing is strictly defined, it's flexible enough to create new material when necessary.

WHAT'S BETTER FOR ME?

With both approaches—living world and living narrative—the PC experience is essentially the same. When they make a decision, the world reacts. The difference is in how the GM experiences the world's story, which is really just a matter of preference.

It's a lot of work to track the events unfolding in a living world. It's also difficult to manipulate story structure and create new ideas in the moment for a living narrative. It's ultimately a question of what you think sounds like more fun.

Mechanics Driven versus Story Driven

We devoted a whole chapter (Chapter 3) to this already! In addition to being a basic concept in understanding how games relate to narrative, it can also be a stylistic choice.

MECHANICS DRIVEN

Mechanics-driven GMing relies on the game system itself as a narrative driver. Rolling on random tables to determine challenges, rewards, and character motivations is an example of mechanics-driven play. It relies on a GM translating game systems into story events.

This approach creates the opportunity for PCs to rely on the game for solutions. If a story concept is represented with game mechanics, players can use the system to interact with it. Mechanics-driven play also shifts some of the decision-making responsibility away from the GM. When rolling on a random encounter table, a GM doesn't actively *decide* to ambush their party—the dice do. The GM just has the responsibility of running the resulting encounter according to their objective.

STORY DRIVEN

This style treats the game system as a tool kit rather than an inflexible structure. Even if a game has rules for resolving combat, it's not necessary to drop into initiative and roll dice unless players are interested in exploring it that way.

A story-driven GM has the flexibility to accommodate ideas that aren't necessarily supported by the system. This style of play puts more options on the table for players too. Assuming characters are more than statistics represented on their sheets, it empowers them to abandon procedure when it gets in the way.

Story-driven play places greater responsibility on the GM. Without the structure of rules, events are directly dictated by their whims. A random encounter with bandits becomes an intentional choice. It's easy for players to take game events personally under these conditions, so be careful.

GMing with Intent

Art may be subjective, but there is definitely a difference between an experienced painter and one who is just starting out. This holds true in GMing too. So how do you improve your skills and master the craft? Part of the answer is learning to act with *intent*.

We know from Chapter 5 on text that information you put into a game becomes the story. We can deliberately shape the story by intentionally manipulating the text. As you grow as a player, you become comfortable with that process.

Similarly, when you grow as a GM, elements of your style become the result of intentional decision-making. GMs make instinctive stylistic choices all the time. When you start out, there really is no other way to do it. Taking the time to examine your choices allows you to evaluate how effective they are.

For example, let's say you secretly lower the difficulty for a PC to pick a lock. As the GM, you ultimately decide how the rules are imposed, so this is a decision you're allowed to make. The players probably won't have a problem with it because this choice benefits them.

Let's take a moment to examine why you made that decision though. Was it to move the game past an unimportant obstacle? If so, why did the PCs need to roll in the first place? After all, the GM dictates when rolls are necessary. Even if there are rules for picking locks, you are not obligated to feature them. Just like you are not bound to a difficulty set by the game designer.

Really, any reason you have to explain your choices *could* be fine. If you understand *why* you make a choice, you have greater mastery over your style. Knowing that you lowered the difficulty of a roll to speed up the game lets you know the roll might not have been important in the first place. The next time you confront your PCs with a lock, you can design a scenario that makes the roll more than an obligation—one where you believe both success and failure are interesting outcomes.

Acting with intent doesn't transform you into a master right away. It just provides you with the opportunity to evaluate your style. Everything else comes with practice.

Schrödinger's Goblins

Every style has strengths and weaknesses, but there is never really a situation that makes something the "wrong" choice. However, styles fall apart when they fail to honor the central contract of collaboration: honoring the contributions of the people you're working with. To better understand this, let's examine the case of Schrödinger's Goblins.

Perhaps you're familiar with the famous thought experiment designed by physicist Erwin Schrödinger in 1935 (the experiment is referred to as Schrödinger's Cat). Schrödinger imagined a cat placed in a box with a container of poison that will, at some point, open, killing the cat. However, the only way we can find out if the poison container has opened is to open the box. Until then, paradoxically, from our point of view the cat is both alive and dead.

Schrödinger's Goblins is a similar thought experiment exploring the nature of storytelling in RPGs. We'll use it to break down stylistic motivations and analyze how they create fun or lead us astray. Seeing these styles applied to a fictional example will help you clarify your own ideas. We're also looking for what "make choices important" asks of us when applied to style.

> *A party of adventurers is faced with a fork in the road. One path leads to safety; the other leads to a dangerous mob of goblins...*

If the party selects the path with an uneventful rest, they'll have more resources and be closer to their goal. If they select the path with the goblins, there will be a fight. The party risks losing resources, but the game will have an action beat.

RPGs are fiction, and the goblins are not really waiting down either path. It is possible to move the goblins to either path for any reason. These goblins don't exist until the GM brings them into the text after the party makes a choice.

To an improvisational GM, the question of how to position these goblins is really a question of the immediate needs of the story. If it feels like the game needs an action scene, goblins—or any other sort of challenge—can appear as needed. If the game needs a downbeat or role-playing scene, the goblins can disappear.

A preparatory GM invests time and effort into crafting a goblin encounter. The encounter needs to be laid out and assigned statistics, which can take hours. Moving the goblins onto whatever path the party chooses means the GM's work isn't wasted—the party *will* fight the goblins. Conversely a preparatory GM could decide the goblins' location *must* be fixed because they have plotted out the road. One path definitely has goblins and the other does not.

To a living world GM the goblins exist as real forces. They don't shift locations unless they have a specific reason to move from one path to another. Swapping them around violates the authenticity of the living world. Encountering the goblins immediately pays off on their existence with an action scene. Passing the goblins by leaves them as a potential problem later on in the game.

TALE AS OLD AS TIME

People have been discussing variations of Schrödinger's Goblins in online RPG forums for years. You can find more perspectives by searching online for "Schrödinger's Encounter" or "The Quantum Ogre."

Living story GMs consider narrative structure and the rhythm of the game in their decision. If this were a written story would goblins appear? Can the goblins serve a narrative purpose? If so, the goblins are free to change positions.

Mechanics-led GMs may have plotted a hexagonal grid map with one hex full of goblins and the other open and empty. They can't really move the goblins because the rules dictate they hold a particular position. They could also have plotted the *chance* to encounter goblins, and a random roll will ultimately decide if and where goblins exist.

HONORING CHOICES

Depending on your style, there could be a clear answer for whether the goblins have a fixed position. However, your style is only a part of the conversation in this situation, because you also have a duty to honor player choices.

If we're GMing with intent, we know that we only need to offer a choice if it matters. If you want to have goblins appear no matter what, you don't need to put a fork in the road. Offering the party a choice and ignoring how it changes results clearly violates "make choices important." Creating a fork in the road to ignore it is at best pointless and at worst undermining collaboration.

This might lead you to ask, If moving goblins invalidates player choices, then aren't styles that motivate you to move them inherently damaging? Not really! As long as you examine your party's goal when they choose a path, and honor that decision, you're still collaborating. For Schrödinger's Goblins, a lot depends on what the PCs know.

The adventurers forge ahead, ready to embrace the fate that awaits them...

If a party doesn't know there could be a goblin encounter ahead, then choosing a path is about something else. If they choose to go north because they know the Tomb of Riches is north and the Desert of Pain is south, then it doesn't matter if both paths potentially have goblins waiting. All it takes to honor their choice in this situation is having the path they chose lead them toward their intended goal.

You can also honor a choice between two paths by creating variation in your goblin encounter. A living story or improvisational GM might feel the narrative calls for action no matter what. However, they can create a distinction in the tone of that action. The north path could have a difficult battle with a band of eight goblins, while the southern path has an easy victory with only four goblins. Although combat against goblins is inevitable in this scenario, the choice still matters because those encounters are *different*.

The ranger returns after scouting the trails ahead. One path has tracks; the other is bare. The party must now make a choice...

Player agency is at risk when the party chooses a path with the intent of avoiding or encountering goblins. If the goblins move in front of the party after the PCs made efforts to avoid them, the GM is actively ignoring their choices.

Styles like living world, which call for keeping the goblins in a fixed place, avoid the issue of potentially violating player choice, but they have other pitfalls. If your party is looking for action, and fails to find it based on an arbitrary choice or random chance, it's worth asking if your style is serving its purpose.

Living worlds are compelling because they provide interesting consequences. Seeing a "realistic" world react helps players feel like their decisions matter. However, if the result of a choice is that nothing happens, then it's worth asking if the living world is really leading to interesting consequences.

Mechanics-led storytelling might hand this question over to randomizers, such as dice. That can be really exciting because risk is present in almost every decision. However, it ultimately places a great deal of trust in forces that don't have an agenda or real understanding of the circumstances at your table. If your party is fatigued by combat or feeling the game is stagnant, adherence to situational rules could be working against you.

The only way to really go astray as a GM is to allow your preference for style to outweigh the input or needs of your fellow players. If you approach your game with intent, and make an effort to value collaboration among the PCs, you'll avoid most pitfalls. Identifying the strengths of other approaches and recognizing the weaknesses of your own will help you grow and refine your process.

Themes

Stories have meaning. It's one of the fundamental assumptions that drive literary analysis. Buried in the events, characters, and scenes of any given novel are insights about society, history, the author's beliefs, and human nature. Sometimes these messages are overtly communicated, as in fables, parables, or fairy tales. Sometimes they are veiled and open to interpretation, as in complex novels, plays, and screenplays. The narrative details that reinforce these ideas are called *themes*.

What Is a Theme?

Put simply, themes shape what a particular story is about.

The relationship between story and theme is symbiotic; they work to support one another. Individual aspects of a piece relate back to central themes to create a feeling of cohesion. When scenes work to support a central theme they make the overall narrative feel stronger, as if it's been constructed on purpose and not randomly. The scene itself feels stronger because it is being elevated by its relationship with the rest of the work.

Along the same lines, a disharmonious relationship between story and theme can hurt a piece. When people talk about something "feeling out of place" in a story, they are struggling to justify an event in terms of their understanding of a story's overall themes. A theme that is insubstantial or unsupported leads people to question what a story is trying to say.

In RPGs, themes are a handy shortcut to making strong fiction. Creating and sustaining themes is how you communicate ideas to your audience. Staying true to themes is how you connect your ideas to a larger story.

Themes in Spontaneous Narrative

Many folks first encounter the idea of themes while studying literature in school. When we read books, stories are presented to us as whole, finished works. Comprehension and interpretation are things that can be evaluated and graded in a classroom. There is an element of inflexibility to our interpretation.

Viewing theme as something that only comes out of finished work warps our perspective. If themes are immutable, they would be fundamentally incompatible with spontaneous creativity. We know that a great deal of what happens at an RPG table is built on the idea of discovery. If you can't plan out how a game session is supposed to go, how can you stay true to a core theme? If a move you make during play isn't made with the intention of supporting a theme, how can we say it's truly related?

It's important to remember all artistic work was once a living process. Authors write, edit, and revise stories. Even with an outline or formula, that process incorporates discovery. There's an old cliché that says "Art is not finished, but abandoned." At a certain point, artists walk away from a piece and declare it "complete." Before the artist says that, it's possible to make changes. Heck, some authors even change their finished work after the fact with new editions or follow-up stories. Which means the idea of something as "complete" or "finished" work is actually arbitrary.

Themes are also generated through the act of interpretation. After an author finishes a story, the audience creates new meaning by relating the work to their own perspective and experience. It's entirely possible for people to discover meaning within a story that the author never intended.

All of that means that themes actually have a *living* relationship with the stories. While events are unfolding, the nature of a story fluctuates. You can create a story to support certain core ideas. You can also discover new ideas as you review what you have already done. It's all part of the same creative process.

Approaching Theme Mechanically

One extremely RPG way to think of theme is as a game mechanic. For narrative gamers, theme is a multitool that helps stories make sense. You can engage theme actively as a guide to drive your story. You can also employ theme retroactively to help you tie ideas together when they don't seem to fit.

In order to use theme this way, you need to accept a single fundamental truth: *your story has meaning.*

As we explained, themes are the meaning behind stories. In order to take advantage of them, you need to believe that your work has meaning. This is true even if you weren't *trying* to create meaning and even if you don't immediately understand what that meaning is.

This philosophy is related to making choices important. If we assume our collaborators add to the story intentionally through making choices, we position ourselves to elevate those choices. Assuming our own work and the overall story have inherent meaning positions us to access theme. You deserve to treat yourself with the same level of respect you give your collaborators. In fact, it works even better if you grant yourself the same respect you show to the artistic heroes who inspire you.

Theme has the potential to touch every aspect of a story. This chapter will break down various incarnations of theme into manageable categories and provide some game mechanics to help you take advantage of them during a game.

PLOT

The plot is simultaneously the core concept of your story and the events that make it up. Your *plot themes* are the overall meaning of your narrative. They explain why everything is happening. They can help you outline what you want to do and justify how events fit together.

Finding a central plot is as simple as answering the question, What is happening? You can sum up most stories with a single sentence. Saying "two people who argue fall in love" tells you the basic plot of *Much Ado about Nothing*. Obviously, there's a lot more to that play than just the core idea. You could tell the story of two people who argue and fall in love without it remotely resembling *Much Ado* (in *The Empire Strikes Back*, for instance).

The sequence of events that tell the core story are also part of the plot. Each scene in a play tells a small story that shapes the larger plot. However, just placing events in order doesn't really give us *Much Ado* either; in fact, it makes the story seem like a confused mess.

A BAD SUMMARY OF *MUCH ADO ABOUT NOTHING*

1. Leonato invites friends over.
2. Claudio and Hero fall in love and plan to get married.
3. Beatrice and Benedick fight.
4. Beatrice and Benedick unknowingly share a connection at a masquerade.
5. Everyone decides it would be a cool idea to trick Beatrice and Benedick into falling in love.
6. The trick works.
7. Don John decides it would be a cool idea to trick Claudio and Hero into falling out of love.
8. Claudio is mean to Hero.
9. Hero's family tricks everyone into believing she is dead.
10. Beatrice acknowledges her love for Benedick but refuses to act on it until someone finds justice for Hero.
11. Don John's plot is revealed.
12. Everyone tricks Claudio into marrying Hero.
13. Benedick and Beatrice also get married.

If this summary seems both confusing and boring, it's because the summary is devoid of theme. We have all the major events that make up the story, but no justification for why they are happening. Plot depends on thematic support to make a story feel logical and natural. Otherwise, events in stories just progress with no other purpose than to reach the end—which is pretty unsatisfying.

You can find themes in your plot by answering another simple question: What ideas make this story interesting?

There can and will be more than one answer. One way to look at storytelling structure is to see a story as a collection of scenes that explore the core themes of the main plot. The scene-by-scene events of the plot are narrative demonstrations of theme.

Deconstructing *Much Ado*, we know some potential answers to the question of what ideas make this story interesting: passion, loyalty, deception, honor, justice, and wit. Focusing on passion enhances this narrative by making the events more dramatic. Whether the characters *really* like to argue or *really* love each other, it's interesting to watch because they're *really* into it.

To explore passion, *Much Ado* puts Beatrice and Benedick in situations that allow us to see their passion from multiple perspectives. Beatrice and Benedick are either at each other's throats with banter or spouting rapturous declarations of devotion.

WHAT'S LOVE GOT TO DO WITH IT?

Shakespearean true believers might notice the absence of major themes like "romance" and "comedy" from this deconstruction. We left those out because they are *genre themes*, something we'll cover a bit later. They define the style of a story. The plot themes we identified are what make the story unique and drive the specific events within it.

The first time we see them together, Beatrice and Benedick clash with an audience to spur them on, showing us their passionate hate makes them the center of attention. They also display passion privately when they discuss their latent feelings in monologues and intimate conversations. Beatrice is so passionate about finding justice for Hero, she rejects the romance at the core of the story. All of these moments are narrative vessels for the core theme.

When we layer on the other themes, the bizarre journey of *Much Ado* starts to make sense. Beatrice and Benedick connecting at a masquerade reveals their potential for romance and helps set the stage for deception being a major form of communication.

It's possible to add new scenes or reframe existing moments and stay true to the plot that defines *Much Ado*, provided the changes we make continue to support core themes. A scene where Don Pedro fails to arouse Beatrice's passion in an argument tells us they are not a good match in a different way than her rejection of his tender advance does. Exchanging heated words is a way to explore passion, but so is exchanging blows! Beatrice and Benedick could be recast as gladiators or wrestlers who express feelings through combat, and their story would still be compelling.

Themes tied to plot reveal the simple mechanics that allow a narrative to function. Having a strong sense of your core themes means you always have a way to make things meaningful.

WORLD
"The world is *more* than a stage, actually."
—*Shakespeare 2*, the more powerful sequel to Shakespeare

A setting is an active participant in the story. The places characters visit, the institutions that guide society, and the physical scenery can all carry thematic weight. A world can contribute to theme through subtle reminders of the kind of space the characters occupy, or by creating overt circumstances characters have to deal with.

Think of a postapocalyptic story. Even if there are no antagonistic characters, the setting will actively challenge protagonists with environmental dangers. Putting characters in the crumbling ashes of an advanced world reminds the audience of what was lost. Before new characters even show up, the world frames how the audience might perceive them. The postapocalyptic genre just wouldn't be the same without the thematic contributions of the world.

Postapocalyptic is an extreme example, but you can see the impact of theme in settings for a multitude of genres. Espionage depends on worlds full of powerful organizations that keep secrets, horror thrives in environments that foster feelings of isolation and helplessness, dungeon-crawling adventure requires dungeons in which to crawl!

To help you use the themes of your world to their fullest potential, we'll create moves that break down the task of using world themes into simple steps. These moves will help you bring the world into the text actively and passively.

SET THE SCENE

Themes can build a physical landscape that makes creating meaningful imagery easy. Highlighting the right themes also signals the mood of a particular scene and allows players to understand what their goals might be. To set the scene choose a theme and pick one of the following moves to make a physical element in the environment:

- A landscape that surrounds characters
- A building that characters use
- An obstacle characters tolerate
- Light that matches tone
- Fragments that hint at a larger story

Let's look at an example in a postapocalyptic game. Park, our GM, is going to have his party face danger as they transport salvaged scrap back to their community. He has identified the core themes for his postapocalyptic world as decay, violence, and resilience. He wants a place that will make a good stage for action, and will remind players of where they are. Physically manifesting themes will give him a perfect stage.

DECAY: A LANDSCAPE THAT SURROUNDS CHARACTERS
Heaps of rusting metal stretch for miles in the Scrap Yard. Decades ago this was a landfill. Now it's a mine for scavengers looking for discarded treasures amongst civilization's refuse. Inside the Scrap Yard you can forget the world is anything but rolling hills of rust.

Since Park wants an action scene, decay won't have much of an active role in events, so Park had it surround his players. Decay is in play even when it's not actively in focus.

VIOLENCE: LIGHT THAT MATCHES TONE
At night in the Scrap Yard, the only light that can be seen comes from the torches and forges of the Diesel Freaks. The sky is red. Forges fill the air with thick smoke that makes breathing difficult and turns the daytime sky a murky orange. It's awful, but it hides the blood stains left by scavengers unfortunate enough to encounter Diesel Freaks in their home territory.

Violence is an active theme that might feel difficult to apply to static elements. Park chose to investigate how his antagonists, the Diesel Freaks, might affect the light. An orange sky and glowing scrap lets the party know this place is dangerous and that violence might be inevitable.

RESILIENCE: FRAGMENTS THAT HINT AT A LARGER STORY
Navigating the Scrap Yard is difficult. Piles shift constantly and unexpectedly, making maps almost useless. The lack of sky cuts off other methods of navigation. Scavengers of various communities aid one another by marking trails and dangers with discreet symbols. They are everywhere if you know what to look for.

This shows that even in a hostile place like the Scrap Yard people still find ways to endure. It also provides tools for the PCs to use in their session. A symbolic language for scavengers solves lots of problems immediately and opens up countless possibilities later.

MAKE THE ENVIRONMENT IMPORTANT

Sometimes the world can have a more direct impact on events of the plot. Your world can actively participate in an action scene, create its own call to action, or make any ongoing event more dramatic. Pick a world theme and choose two of the following:

- [Theme] threatens someone's physical safety.
- [Theme] makes a plan more complicated than before.
- [Theme] prompts a mechanical benefit or setback.
- [Theme] adds emotional weight to an action.

Your selected prompts will help you choose how to make your world theme active.

Here's a scenario to illustrate action in the world of the Scrap Yard: Rax (played by Ramon) and Thrasher (played by Yuki) are facing off against a gang of Diesel Freaks. Thrasher is trying to buy time while Rax takes their stash of salvage to safety. It's the perfect time for a theme of the world to add spice to an already exciting scene.

Rax is climbing some junk, which is a little less cool than swinging a bat full of nails. Our world themes can change that! Since violence is already present in this combat, let's focus on decay. We'll have decay threaten someone's safety to add emotional weight to this climb. The easiest way to do that is to threaten Thrasher:

Park (GM): *As Rax climbs the tower of ancient rusting steel, zie hears the telltale groan of scrap starting to shift. Zie spots a tormented cluster of concrete and rebar ready to fall. Rax can easily avoid it, but it's going to fall right toward Thrasher.*

Decaying scrap made Rax's climb part of the fight for Thrasher's life. Using the world themes, Park managed to create active action roles for both of his PCs!

You can also take advantage of this move as a PC. Thrasher is on the ground trying to keep the Diesel Freaks off the scrap. She could just swing her bat, but Yuki realizes she can honor the world by drawing on Resilience, and she petitions for a mechanical advantage.

Yuki: *Instead of just attacking, I want to draw the Diesel Freaks under the scrap that's currently threatening me.*

Park (GM): *Okay, that's pretty cool, but the Freaks come up in initiative before the scrap falls. You might take a hit.*

Yuki: *Thrasher has been taking hits since the day she crawled out of the heap.*

Thrasher is still a central part of the action because we're exploring how tough she really is, but now there's a spotlight on Rax, too, because hir actions directly influenced how the scene played out. All of that upholds the tone of the world while making it an active part of the narrative.

Referencing a detail in your world's environment can emphasize active themes in an ongoing scene, incorporate a desired theme without overcomplicating ongoing events, or set expectations by foreshadowing impending events. To make this move, select a theme and bring a piece of the environment into focus using that theme to shape your perspective.

If you're passively drawing on a theme all you need to do is select a [theme] and:

- **Underscore:** This uses imagery to emphasize themes actively at play in a scene. Underscoring supports a tone and ties a place to a moment. The same environment can convey different meanings depending on the needs of the scene.
- **Reflect:** This ties in inactive themes through imagery. It can help transition into a new scene while providing a sense of thematic continuity. Reflecting helps establish a relationship between characters and the events driven by their world.
- **Foreshadow:** This creates imagery to transition out of a scene and gets players thinking about what's coming next. Having one tone can make a game feel dull or overwhelming. Tying positive imagery into negative moments can help a scene feel varied even if it's mostly concerned with a single subject.

After escaping a desperate fight, Rax and Thrasher sit side-by-side in front of a campfire.

UNDERSCORE: DECAY
Park (DM): *Exhausted, your scavengers take a moment to feel the warmth of the fire. The bullet holes in the steel at your back cast a shadow on the concrete wall behind you. The Scrap Yard traps Rax and Thrasher's silhouettes in a thin web of jagged edges.*

After the action scene, Park wants to emphasize that the encounter really meant something. The fight is over, but Rax and Thrasher haven't left the Scrap Yard yet. This image lets everyone muse on how they're still in its clutches.

REFLECT: VIOLENCE
The smell of burning wood slowly overpowers the odor of gunpowder but illuminates the drying bloodstains spattered across Thrasher's armor.

This reflection balances the relative peace of a campfire against the difficult journey that brought them to it. Calling out the blood stains enables Ramon and Yuki to reflect on their character's physical state. It might even prompt the PCs to physically wash away the events of the previous scene.

FORESHADOW: RESILIENCE
The flames eat away at the wood in the pit. Logs shrink into scarred ashen versions of themselves, but their structure holds. They do not break.

This foreshadows some hope in the postcombat bleakness. The fire of the Scrap Yard has worn Rax and Thrasher, but it did not kill them.

CHARACTER
Almost all RPGs are ensemble fiction. Lots of stories in other media focus on a single principal character backed by a supporting cast. RPGs have multiple primary protagonists sharing the stage, and usually no one character is more important than the others. This makes the thematic landscape rich and also complex.

Each character has *personal themes* that define their story in addition to a relationship with the central themes of your narrative. RPG parties experience many successes and failures together, but thematic diversity means that not all moments carry the same meaning for every character. Sometimes thematic overlap means investigating multiple perspectives on the same subject.

Weaving character themes with story themes might seem daunting. After all, it's a lot of information to manage. However, it's actually a great way to keep your game feeling varied and multifaceted.

In a horror game, constantly focusing on fear actually lessens the impact of terrifying moments. Character themes give us something to care about and add stakes to moments of peril. Themes such as guilt, debt, and loneliness can keep a private investigator on a case they know they should leave alone. They also help an audience connect when supernatural circumstances make a story difficult to relate to. Well-supported character themes can change "Only an idiot would open that door" to "Oh no! I can't believe they have to open that door!"

GENRE

Every storytelling genre has core themes that define it. In an RPG, genre themes help you maintain your tone and stay true to your objective. They act like trails to guide you and your fellow players through chaotic landscapes rich with possibilities. Engaging with a genre theme reminds everyone what you are doing and helps make a new story feel familiar.

This actually makes genre themes less critical than the other theme types. Themes based around plot, character, and world define your story's unique voice. Genre is a passive tool; it informs how you stylistically explore critical themes as they arise.

If a game is an automobile your plot themes are the engine that provides the power, character themes are the wheels that allow it to move, your world is the frame that holds everything together, and your genre is the body and paint that make it recognizable as a car. Genre's not critical to make your story work, but it will make it nice to look at.

From a utilitarian perspective, genre themes can patch rough areas where things feel out of place or underdeveloped. They can't fix a broken story, but they help people overlook structural problems while you sort out complicated mechanics.

THEMATIC STATS

Take a character in your game and decide on five themes that define their personal story. Then write out the three most prominent campaign themes for your game. Distribute 15 points to the character themes you listed based on how closely they relate to your campaign themes, with a higher number meaning a stronger thematic relationship.

✏️ **Write down your character themes:**

✏️ **Write down your core campaign themes:**

Many games already have mechanical support for genre themes built into their design. If you pick up a horror, sci-fi, or fantasy RPG, it has tools to structure stories within its associated genre. It's still possible to feel lost during a game. As a PC sometimes your course of action is unclear or there are too many good options. As a GM sometimes the game on the table doesn't match the vision in your head.

PATCH QUESTIONS

When you find a storytelling problem, genre can slap an aesthetic patch on things. This keeps the game together so you can move on or sort out solutions. Answering these questions as a PC or GM can help you sidestep problems by calling on themes that feel generally true to your aesthetic:

- If this were a movie, what would happen next?
- What's the most common tool used by characters in this genre? How can you use it here?
- Which outside forces typically intervene in moments like this?
- Where is the most logical place to jump to skip past this moment?
- What always makes characters strong in moments like this?
- Is there a typical or immediate problem that can take focus so you can come back to this?

Imagery

Imagery is figurative language or evocative visuals in literature and film. Normally it's something people associate with literary or film criticism. Folks who create in games rarely think about imagery as something in their tool kit. Whether we acknowledge it or not imagery still appears in our games. Understanding it allows us to take advantage of something we're already doing, and enhances the game.

As a player, imagery can help you build a more distinct identity for your character and lend greater significance to your actions. As a GM imagery can help you maintain a strong tone for your game world and help you communicate ideas to your players indirectly. For everyone imagery allows for more nuanced communication that's effective whether people understand what you are doing or not. It also helps add some flavor to descriptions of game events, which makes playing more interesting.

What Does Imagery Look Like in a Game?

Imagery links larger themes and meaning to descriptive elements in your game world. Symbols used in imagery are signifiers of a larger storytelling agenda behind smaller moments we explore at the table.

Let's say we're playing Sheila, an older knight with a complicated past. She's tough and strong because she's been through hell, but it's starting to wear on her. Obviously when we introduce her, we can point that out to the group. However, as the game progresses she'll be working alongside her younger partymates and facing the same challenges. In terms of the game, challenges will affect her the same way they do her comrades. Her hit points will move up and down like everyone else's. To keep the personality of her character concept we'll have to distinguish her experience through description. Using imagery we can make that process colorful and fun.

First, let's look at some actions for Sheila without imagery:

- *Sheila's Intimidate roll is 15! She looms over the bouncer, taking advantage of her size to subtly carry a threat.*
- *Sheila bashes the goblin with her shield and does 8 points of damage!*
- *Sheila's armor class is 16, so the attack misses.*

That's all fine, but it misses the core of Sheila's character and doesn't really showcase her personality. Creating imagery around a piece of Sheila's equipment will allow us to convey the same information with more personality:

- *Sheila's Intimidate roll is 15! She casually plants her heavy shield on the ground with a thud. The torchlight dances off countless dents and scratches on its surface. The bouncer can tell Sheila's been in a few fights and that she wouldn't mind another.*
- *There's a heavy clang as Sheila slams her battered shield into the goblin, doing 8 points of damage.*
- *Sheila's armor class is 16, so the spear crashes against her shield, adding a new scratch but failing to do any lasting damage.*

The shield, like Sheila herself, has been through hell. The dents and scratches on it mirror her checkered past, and its durability mirrors her strength. When we reference the shield we can emphasize these aspects of Sheila's character without pulling focus away from the action. Establishing this connection can help us touch on these themes even without the shield literally moving the action. Let's say Sheila just makes a knowledge check to identify something from her past:

> *"I recognize that seal. It's from my old combat unit. I didn't leave on the best terms."*

That's definitely got Sheila's personality, and it tells everyone what they need to know. However, using the imagery from the shield we can make it play out with more dramatic flair:

Sheila falls silent as she studies the seal. Light from the campfire dances across the ancient dents on her shield. "Yeah, I've seen this before. I used to work with them."

The same imagery can be used to convey different meanings depending on the circumstances under which it appears. Earlier we used the damage on the shield to emphasize how tough Sheila is, but her age is also a part of her story. The same image that told us she is tough can tell us she's getting worn out:

An anguished metallic creak accompanies the rising and falling of Sheila's chest under her labored breath. The damaged metal scrapes against loose bolts struggling to hold true. It stayed together this time, only barely.

Once meaning has been established for a particular image, you can send a strong message by breaking that pattern. If we usually see Sheila's shield weather punishment, it really means something when we say it has suffered damage.

Despite its name, imagery doesn't have to be tied to visual phenomena. You can create imagery with any well-defined piece of sensory information. Sounds, smells, and feelings can all help carry themes through imagery. We could use the smell of coal and oil to communicate the harsh indifference of industrialization in a steampunk setting:

- The man screams, clutching his hand as the machine drones on undaunted. You cannot even smell the blood over the thick aroma of coal and oil.

- The child looks up at you as they silently hold out a soot-stained palm. You can smell a faint trace of coal and oil coming from their clothes.
- The Baron clinks your glass in celebration. Even the domineering peaty burn of the fine whiskey fails to hide smell of coal and oil floating in the Baron's office.

All of this works to build a picture in the minds of the folks you are playing with. Reinforcing who your character is makes it easier for your fellow players to understand what you want out of the game. Imagery is just one way to further that conversation.

How Do I Create Imagery?

Let's create some imagery through an exercise. Fill in the blanks and answer the questions below to build an image that you can take into one of your games.

STEP 1: PICK THEMES

Choose three core ideas you want to communicate through an abstract image. You can always layer more meaning onto an image once it's created, but it's always best to start out with something simple.

✎ **My themes are:**

Consider themes that relate to the tone and setting of your game. If you are running a cyberpunk thing like Corporate Oligarchy, oppression and corruption are going to be key themes. If you're running a Western you might want to consider themes like desperation, justice, and revenge. Ask yourself what in your world you find most interesting and what you want your players to feel when they are there. Building imagery around core themes will help your game world look and feel cohesive.

Most of the imagery you create as a player will be related to your character. What are the most interesting and important things about them? What do they care about? What do they aspire to? Any of those questions can help you find a core theme. A core theme doesn't have to be something your character is concerned with all the time; it just has to be important to them in an abstract sense.

STEP 2: PICK A FOCUS

Next you'll need to choose a literal image to be central to your metaphor. For the sake of simplicity, we'll call this a focus.

A good focus is strongly tied to one of the five senses. Imagery is often oriented visually, but your focus can be anything folks can easily picture in their minds. It can be simple like a skull, the smell of cinnamon, or the caw of a crow.

As you get comfortable with focuses, you can explore more complicated ones like the reflection caused by light hitting gold, the unpleasant sensation of a metal spoon scraping your teeth, or the feeling of waiting in silence to hear an unfamiliar noise a second time.

No matter what you choose you want to be able to sum it up in a single sentence. The more difficult your focus is to express, the harder it will be to use in the game.

✏ **My focus will be:**

ORDINARY IS EXTRAORDINARY

You'll want to work with something that's unremarkable on its own; this will allow the themes you impose to be more prominent in your narration. The chime of a bell doesn't mean much on its own, so you are free to tie all sorts of meanings to it. It can be associated with danger by having it signal the rounds of an oppressive inquisition, or it can mean luck and success ringing in jackpots at a casino. If you select something that carries its own significance, be aware of what that is so you can work with it, or take care to be clear about how you are subverting it.

STEP 3: CONNECT YOUR THEMES TO YOUR FOCUS

Ideally, your focus should have a clear relationship to your themes. The process of creating imagery involves constantly asking yourself, How are these ideas related? Sometimes the answer to that question is fairly straightforward. Looking at the example that follows, rats are related to fear because some people think they are scary.

Sometimes you have to work harder to connect a theme to a focus. Let's say our focus is "the unknown." Rats themselves are not particularly mysterious, so we'll have to work harder to connect them to the unknown. Rats aren't exactly enigmatic, but they are small; they see things people don't. Their connection to the unknown could be "Rats live in places we can't see." (We revisit the rats example later in the chapter.)

✏️ **Tie each core theme to your focus:**

1. My focus is connected to:

   ----

   because:

   ----

2. My focus is connected to:

   ----

   because:

   ----

3. My focus is connected to:

   ----

   because:

STEP 4: EXPLORE CONNECTIONS THROUGH SCENES

Now that you understand how your imagery connects to your themes, it's time to build a tool kit of images that tie your focus to the five senses. Understanding how your focus relates to different senses will help you use it effectively in many different situations.

SIGHT

- In what places are people likely to encounter your focus? How can those connect to your themes?
- What specific visual details about your focus relate to your themes?
- How can your focus appear in the abstract?

- Are there any visual clues that hint at the presence of your focus indirectly?

SOUND
- What sounds do you associate with your focus?
- How can someone's voice bring your focus to mind?
- What sounds can your focus make indirectly?

TOUCH
- How would touching your focus make you feel?
- What sort of things does your focus touch?
- What detailed textures does your focus possess that relate to your themes?
- Could your focus cause pain?

TASTE
- If your focus is a living thing, how do you feel about what it eats? Do any of those emotions connect to your themes?
- If your focus is a living thing, in what contexts is it eaten?
- If your focus was on a logo for a brand of food, what food would you expect to see it paired with? What would be surprising or upsetting?

SMELL
- Does your focus have a scent?
- Do the environments in which a person might find your focus have any scents associated with them?
- What bodily reaction would you have to smelling something that is part of your focus?

STEP 5: TIE SENSE TO ACTION
Finally, take the sense-based images you created and tie them to actions that might occur in games. The more actions you can weave elements of your focus into, the more versatile your imagery will be as a storytelling tool.

✎ **Incorporate your focus into descriptions of the following potential game elements:**

An Attack:

A Chase:

A Room at a Hotel or Inn:

Something Valuable:

An NPC You Might Encounter:

EXAMPLE

This example follows the five steps to creating imagery that we discussed in this section.

STEP 1: PICK THEMES

Death

Fear

The Unknown

STEP 2: PICK A FOCUS

My focus will be rats.

STEP 3: CONNECT YOUR THEMES TO YOUR FOCUS

Rats are connected to death because they eat carrion and contribute to decay.

Rats are connected to fear because people think they are scary.

Rats are connected to the unknown because they live in places we cannot see.

STEP 4: EXPLORE CONNECTIONS THROUGH SCENES

SIGHT

Rats live in dark places that people consider dirty.

People fear the dark and things we can't see are unknown.

Rodent eyes can appear to glow in the dark, so a bunch of rats can appear as a spooky glowing swarm.

Rats can be depicted in art like tattoos, graffiti, or old woodcuts.

SOUND

Rats can hiss and squeak. They also make scratching and bumping sounds when moving about.

Rats are light but if they swarm you can hear the thudding of their soft footsteps.

TOUCH

Rats can scratch and bite if they feel trapped.

TASTE

Rats are scavengers that eat carrion and trash.
I think that's gross! That ties in to fear pretty easily.

SMELL

The places I imagine I will find rats are damp,
musty, and rotten. When I think of them I think of
sewers, attics, and basements. The air feels
dangerous and crawling.

STEP 5: TIE SENSE TO ACTION

- An Attack:

  Like a cornered rat the cultist suddenly turns and
  lashes out with a jerky animalistic strike.

- A Chase:

  You choke on cold musty air that smells faintly of rot
  as you bolt down the narrow passageway. You can
  hear the scraping of something with clawed feet
  following close behind you.

- A Room at a Hotel or Inn:

  As you look out the window of your motel the lights of the city lose shape and focus. They become the beady eyes of a thousand hungry rats watching you for a sign of weakness.

- Something Valuable:

  The sack bulges with stacks of angular bills. You can only guess at how much is inside, but it's surely more than you've ever seen collected in a single place. It almost appears to writhe with many moving bodies as it dangles in your employer's tight grip.

- An NPC You Might Encounter:

  His laugh washes over you in a series of hideous nasal squeaks. You can't help but notice his features come to a rodent-like point as he flashes a wicked smile.

Now That I Have an Image I Like, How Do I Use It?

The secret to using imagery at the table is repetition. This is true whether you are a player or a GM. Your goal with imagery is to connect themes to something people can appreciate through their senses. You establish that connection through patterns.

Every time you reference an image, you give it power and significance. The more frequently an image appears, the stronger its association with your themes becomes. This means all you have to do to create meaningful imagery is keep returning to certain images in your narration. A black hat on its own means nothing. If the primary antagonist of your game wears a black hat, seeing one hanging from the wall becomes exciting.

When an author or filmmaker creates imagery they do it with a cohesive plan in mind. They go back and edit their stories to highlight moments that underscore their story's central themes. RPGs are improvised, so we don't really have the luxury of cutting content to highlight the most relevant parts. However, we get something even better—we get to cheat!

Repeating an image establishes a connection. That means you can create imagery accidentally, or without much forethought, by calling back to something that happened earlier in the game. You don't need to plan ahead to introduce something as important imagery; you can simply gravitate to what feels important after you start playing around with it.

The other advantage we have as role players is the nature of memory. After four hours at the table people tend to walk away with only a few highlights of the session still in their minds. You don't need everything you say in the game to feel like tightly written prose. Referring to your imagery just a handful of times each session will be enough to establish your connections and make your game more flavorful.

If you want to experiment with imagery, use this chart to help guide you. Try to refer to your imagery three times each gaming session. Check a box each time you feel like you succeeded!

IMAGERY CHART

My themes are:

My focus is:

Images:

O Sight   O Sound   O Smell   O Taste   O Touch

Progress:

Playing to Change

GMs carry a great deal of creative responsibility, but it's also easier for them to adapt wisdom from other fields to their craft. Most academic advice on storytelling assumes an author has total control over the fiction. It also assumes an audience format that's extremely different from RPGs. This puts PC players in an interesting place: how can you learn from literature if the way you create and portray characters is fundamentally different?

In this chapter we'll examine common literary structures for heroic characters to see what is and isn't relevant for RPGs. Then we'll explore some methods for making PCs as dynamic and compelling as literary protagonists.

The Classic Hero

You might have learned about the classic hero in school when discussing story structures such as the "hero's journey" or Joseph Campbell's "monomyth." In case you didn't, the basic idea is that many heroic narratives have a similar structure. A character leaves home, goes on a journey, and returns changed. At its core, the monomyth is about change and the process of becoming a hero. Characters undertaking the hero's journey start in a place of humble stability, endure trials, and emerge as heroes.

A good deal of the foundational literature that inspired RPGs is deeply enmeshed in the monomyth. Many games even have mechanics based on concepts within this structure. Games in which PCs acquire experience points (XP) to grow in power are structured to represent the idea of the journey, slowly making characters more capable. A knight might start out struggling to overcome bandits and end up trading blows with a dragon.

Despite the popularity of the monomyth, it's difficult to apply to most gaming experiences. Monomyth focuses on a single protagonist and what makes their journey exceptional. It's certainly possible to play a game where a single PC takes the spotlight while others act as a supporting cast, but it requires a group enthusiastic about the idea.

Folks who reject the idea of games as art often point to the monomyth as a justification for their position. The monomyth does not fit the RPG format, they argue, therefore stories built with RPGs don't hold legitimacy.

SCHOOL'S OUT FOREVER

It's important to understand that the monomyth isn't necessary for creating a good character. We promise Joseph Campbell won't break into your home to chastise you for making the hero the wrong way.

Remember that monomyth is nothing more than an analytical format. The idea of the monomyth exists for simplicity's sake. It strips away the complexity of heroic narratives to find the basic structure at their core. Those who choose to follow monomythic structure in their writing use it as a guide to focus a narrative and make it fall in line with a particular style. Focusing on a single character is just a stylistic choice.

RPG storytelling exists for the sake of fun. If you want a table full of heroes, you don't need to follow the classic hero's journey format. Most RPGs are ensemble fiction, stories where a cast of characters with individual journeys all contribute to the plot. Juggling multiple monomyths can make a game feel unfocused and even repetitive.

Monomyth ironically clashes with the power fantasy at the heart of many RPGs. Most of the hero's journey is focused on *becoming* empowered and heroic. Part of the appeal of certain games is casting yourself in an empowered heroic role. Huge sections of the mono-myth are just part of the background.

The Iconic Hero

Most PCs have a different heroic structure to their stories. *Iconic heroes* are confronted with an ever-expanding number of problems and rely on key heroic strengths to overcome challenges. They are driven by flexible heroic motivations that call them to action in a variety of circumstances.

An iconic hero *may* have an overarching story with a beginning and an end. However, some don't have defined ends to their stories at all. Plenty of iconic heroes appear as protagonists in stories totally unrelated to their core plot.

Modern serialized fiction like franchise films, serial novels, TV programs, and comic books make frequent use of this heroic structure. Comic book superheroes in particular have helped mold the iconic form. Many superhero characters have definitive origins but no real end to their stories. They exist to have countless adventures, driven by versatile motivations.

Iconic heroes aren't invested in *becoming*; they already *are*. Tales of iconic heroes presume victory that may or may not depend on growth or change. In fact, an aspect to the iconic structure requires a hero's ability to return to core strengths and weaknesses at the end of each adventure to leave room for new stories.

RPGs draw on iconic structure heavily, especially in long-form campaigns. Parties of adventurers are given diverse skills and enough motivation to keep them traveling as a group. They have the capacity to take on an incredible range of problems, and the fun is in seeing how they handle new situations.

Although iconic structure fits RPGs more comfortably than monomyth, it's not helpful to treat it as an inflexible foundation. The iconic structure is utilitarian; it allows a character to be incorporated into a number of stories but not necessarily be dramatically affected by those stories. Iconic characters *do* experience emotional arcs, but they rarely exhibit transformative growth. This creates a reliable personality and enables multiple authors to tell different stories that all feel true to the character. In a way, it means the iconic structure resists growth.

There is no need to apply this kind of limitation to PCs. In fact, it hurts your ability to meaningfully react to the stories your character participates in. It *is* fun to play a character who remains consistent from adventure to adventure, but avoiding personal growth takes away some of your storytelling tools. Also, it unintentionally reduces the importance of the narrative by preventing it from having an impact.

Dynamic Play

Classic heroes are always on a growth trajectory because they are moving toward a final form. Not everything your character experiences during a game is growth though, and PCs don't have defined endings. For RPGs, it's better to think in terms of movement rather than growth.

In improv, performers are taught to approach each scene as a window into a critical moment in a character's life. Adopting this philosophy helps ensure that the scenes presented to the audience feel significant. It assumes there is a reason we are focusing on that particular moment. To make this work, performers need to *play to be affected*.

When you play a character to be affected, you assume the events in your game's text are inherently important to your character's story. This is an extension of the "make choices important" philosophy. It adds the overall game's narrative to your agenda when dealing with the immediate challenge of reacting to the ideas of your collaborators. It's about allowing the story to change your PC in order to make events feel significant.

Change shouldn't mean giving up what you love about a character. The dictum aimed at writers that you should "kill your darlings" is a philosophy for people who don't have to live in a character's skin for a few hours every week. Let's look at some approaches to play that you can take without losing what you care about.

TRANSFORMATION

Improvisers say scenes end with *transformation*, a character experiencing a change or just an event having a meaningful impact on them. Characters open to change are inherently easier to create story beats for than characters who are resistant to change. Changes can be small and still have meaning. Shifting relationships, emotional states, and goals are all transformations a character can undergo while on a larger story arc.

BE CHALLENGED

PCs face all sorts of peril on their journeys. The general expectation is they'll overcome obstacles and eventually triumph. Unless you're playing a very specific type of game, the GM generally confronts you with solvable problems. The game system ensures that you have tools to address those problems.

If we're playing to be challenged, we know that the obstacles facing our character are *important.* Ideally, they are important to the character specifically. As a PC, the battles you fight, puzzles you solve, and wrongs you right say something about you. Those events become more important if we can convince our audience that your character is being challenged.

This isn't a question of probability. Your character has strengths, and you're most likely taking on challenges that highlight those strengths. It's recognizing that even when you are likely to succeed, there is something about the challenge that makes it worthy of your character's attention. That can be the stakes of the situation, your emotional commitment to your beliefs, or even just that the challenge reinforces critical information about who you are.

Travis is playing Gearhead, a character built to specialize in electrical and mechanical engineering. He's currently disarming a bomb. It's an easy role for him, but this challenge is in the game for a reason. Primarily it's part of the GM's effort to support Travis's character choice. However, it can also say something important about who Gearhead is. Travis can redirect a scene about succeeding or failing to focus on what makes Gearhead cool and competent by recognizing why his character is suited to the task.

1. **Travis:** *Gearhead looks over the wires that make up the interior of the bomb and says, "Ugh, these things never look as neat as they do in training."*
2. **Travis:** *Gearhead takes a breath and lets the chaotic world around him fade away. He traces the tangled paths of the wires and silently curses the fact that he doesn't have the opportunity to check his work. Snip.*
3. **Travis:** *Before Gearhead cuts his chosen wire a vision of failure gives him pause. Friends and family lost; goals unachieved. "Not today."*
4. **Travis:** *Gearhead steals a glance over to his sergeant, still annoyed about getting chewed out earlier. "It'd serve you right if I got us all blown up."*

All of those takes highlight the importance of the moment without sacrificing Gearhead's competence. The first and second draw attention to his training and ability to focus. The third and fourth incorporate character flaws that aren't currently hindering him but still define his character.

Being challenged also involves reading your GM's objective. Lots of challenges exist to explore your party's competence, but there are moments when GMs are looking to establish important ideas about NPCs or forces in the game world. It's common for heroes to banter or put on a brave face. Sometimes this is welcome; sometimes it robs significance from critical pieces of the narrative.

This aspect of being challenged plays into the idea of sharing focus. Identifying when it's your time to shine goes hand-in-hand with identifying when a moment calls for your support. Accepting that a threat is challenging can be subtle and doesn't require you to sacrifice your status. Let's break down a few examples:

Rejecting Challenge	Accepting Challenge	Analysis
GM: *"I've absorbed the power of three crystals already. No being alive can hope to stop me."* **PC:** *"Shut up, I'm gonna kill you."* *I attack.*	**GM:** *"I've absorbed the power of three crystals already. No being alive can hope to stop me!"* **PC:** *"It's a real shame those crystals didn't also make you the strong silent type."* *I cautiously look for new dangers before I attack.*	Both of these scenes involve a PC telling the boss they talk too much. Example 2 keeps the banter but takes a moment to draw attention to the fact that the PC still takes the fight seriously.
GM: *"No one has ever come out of the Doom Maze alive."* **PC:** *"Oh, good, it looks like we're finally allowed to go in. I thought we'd have to sign a waiver."*	**GM:** *"No one has ever come out of the Doom Maze alive."* **PC:** *I look at the door and back to the gate-keeper "I am Captain Vale. I just want to be sure you remember in case I forget to tell you when we come back out."*	In Example 1 the PC completely dismisses the threat of the Doom Maze. It establishes the character won't care when they succeed. Example 2 establishes that the character understands the Doom Maze is a threat, is confident they'll succeed, and that their success will matter.

Rejecting Challenge	Accepting Challenge	Analysis
GM: *"This has gone on long enough. It is time you lay down your blade. You have made a mockery of your clan's name."* **PC:** *I don't even wait for him to finish before I attack.*	**GM:** *"This has gone on long enough. It is time you lay down your blade. You have made a mockery of your clan's name."* **PC:** *I don't hear his words. All I can think about is the corruption he has wrought. When people talk about this moment they will say I struck him down without remorse. That I never loved my clan. That I did not fear death. In this moment I feel all of those things, but they are not strong enough to stay my blade.*	In this moment the GM is offering the player an opportunity to commit to their choices. Example 1 definitely signals that the PC is firm in their beliefs. Example 2 manages to do that while still acknowledging that the decision to attack is difficult. It also adds power to the moment by implying that people will talk about it.

Accepting challenge allows you to hold on to everything that makes your character cool and competent without taking power from the ideas of other players.

BE VULNERABLE

Most folks see heroes as defined by what makes them invulnerable. Most of the stuff you put on a character sheet is information about how cool and special they are. To a certain extent you want to approach your game with the intent to indulge that aspect of your character. However, if your focus is entirely built around your character's strengths, there is a danger that they will feel flat.

A character who is not vulnerable to events around them will not change. This is not *necessarily* a liability. There are plenty of stories that revolve around characters staying constant and moving the world around them. Stories with iconic heroes do this frequently. However, closing off access to transformative events puts a tremendous amount of pressure on every other aspect of the story. If you're playing for narrative strength, it makes things easier to keep your options open.

We already know how vulnerability can be an asset to us as storytellers. Vulnerability in characters allows the plot to move. Vulnerabilities open us up to heartbreak, humiliation, and failure. Those are a nightmare in the real world, but in a story they create conflict that drives the plot.

Let's look at a character who's just been put in a vulnerable position. Jacinto, a brash pilot, has just been confronted by his allies about his alcoholism:

Jacinto: *"I don't have a drinking problem, and I don't want to talk about it!" He walks away.*

This is a pretty natural reaction to that kind of criticism. It's a move to avoid a difficult conversation and protect the character's sensitivity. However, it also stops the scene entirely. There's no possibility to explore the space because the character shuts down the conversation before it starts. This could be a part of a larger story that's building, but the immediate result is no change in the character.

Jacinto: *"I don't know how to stop."*

This is a natural but fully vulnerable response. This kind of reaction to confrontation signals a pivot in the storyline. Admitting to a problem, and confronting it, takes a tremendous amount of vulnerability. The scene that follows is going to put heavy focus on serious truths about the character.

This kind of honesty is a pretty big dramatic beat. If the character isn't ready for a critical change, heavy vulnerability will move their story too much. There is plenty of middle ground for this character.

> **Jacinto:** *"I don't have a drinking problem! I drink when I get upset, or when I feel bored, or when I have too much to do, or when I have access to alcohol!"*

> **Jacinto:** *"Obviously I have a problem! It's a cry for help, and frankly it's taken you way too long to point it out!" Jacinto defiantly takes another swig from his flask.*

Both of these responses make the character vulnerable enough to exist in a conversation about his drinking, but he is still resistant to change. They also keep the tone light, communicating the following scene will not be a heavy confrontation.

Improvisers are taught to create vulnerable characters for scenes and possess vulnerability as performers on the stage. Vulnerability allows a character to be affected by what happens to them. That in turn makes it easier to pursue a scene as a moment critical to their character, and therefore important enough to share with an audience.

HOW DO I USE VULNERABILITY WITH A STRONG CHARACTER?

Most folks associate vulnerability with being emotionally fragile. A character doesn't have to cry at the drop of a hat to be vulnerable; they just have to care about what's going on and react as though it matters. The most enduring iconic heroes are built with a set of values or beliefs that allow them to invest themselves in their adventures.

To help you establish a utilitarian vulnerability, recognize your motivation by asking yourself, *Why do I care?* Answering this question for your character gives them a reason to invest in a given scene. Ideally your answer is emotionally grounded and personal, such as:

- This will help me find my father.
- I can't live with myself if I run away.
- This job is the only thing I don't hate about myself.

It's okay to start with more general motivations, such as:

- I'm dedicated to the greater good.
- This will make me rich.
- I hate demons.

Broad and impersonal motivations are a good place to start, but you'll have more success if you go deeper. You can make a broad motivation more personal by asking, *Why is that important to me?* The more emotional weight you put into your motivation, the greater your potential for creating vulnerability. Compare these examples to see how you might strengthen your vulnerability potential:

Okay	Great
I'm dedicated to the greater good because I've trained all my life to pursue it.	I care about the greater good because I have seen what happens when other people don't care.
I want to be rich to get out of debt.	I want to be rich because I'm afraid of the people I owe.
I want to destroy evil.	Demons used to make me feel afraid and I want to prove they don't anymore.

Motivations set you up for success, but they aren't direct actionable goals. To make role-playing vulnerability easier, you can create objectives based on your emotional motivations. To do this take your motivation and ask, *How do I prove it?*

Let's use this method to make an iconic hero who appears to be detached able to meaningfully interact with a story. Brock "The Black Scorpion" Hardstone is an ex–special forces badass running from his past. He wants to keep people at a distance because he's afraid they'll get hurt.

Brock doesn't want to fight weapons smugglers in an abandoned subway tunnel. Part of his strategy to avoid situations like that is simply closing himself off from people. In order for the story to work, we need him to care about something more than he dislikes his past.

Here are some possible motivations that will make him vulnerable enough to move the story:

- I keep my promises.
- The kids in this neighborhood deserve a better shot than I had.
- I used to be a bad guy, and I regret it.

Those are really broad ideas that could lead to Brock intervening in a situation he probably wants to stay out of. It will be lots of fun watching the chaos that follows his decision to step in. That's just the surface level, though. It only lets things move forward.

Taking a motivation and making it important will provide the character with dramatic depth. A tough guy who pushes people away has less going for him than a tough guy who keeps what he cares about close. If Brock has sworn to keep his promises because "he broke a promise once and it destroyed his life," there's suddenly more weight behind everything he does.

CHARACTERS FIRST

Having a motivation that revolves around relationships between characters is easier to use than one that's based on plot points. Having a character vulnerability that involves other characters makes the actions of PCs and NPCs important to your story by default. Being able to explore vulnerability through dialogue allows you to play more actively.

If Brock promised Annie Freeman—a streetwise tween who got herself mixed up in all this—he'd keep her safe, it suddenly really matters if she gets hurt. It transforms an incidental game event (a character taking damage) into an iconic character moment.

That motivation adds to the game no matter how Brock's player decides to use it. Wading into the fight to end things quickly, dropping to his knees and shouting "Noooooooo!" or apologizing to Annie after the fight is over all honor the vulnerability and make the events of the story more significant.

Looking for Trouble

In most media the audience is set up to root for the protagonists. The nature of storytelling makes the life of a protagonist fraught. When the hero is in danger or makes a bad decision it's natural to think *Oh my goodness, don't do that!* Wanting to see someone succeed goes hand-in-hand with wanting to insulate them from danger.

In an RPG, the audience has the power to actually step in and guide the protagonists away from misfortune. That instinct can make your job as a storyteller difficult. Some really compelling moments in fiction come out of characters acting against their best interests.

In this chapter we'll look at how letting characters get themselves into trouble can actually make the game more fun. First, let's take a look at why most people *don't* play this way.

Playing Protectively

Playing protectively is making decisions primarily for the benefit of your PC. This means both advancing their agenda and keeping them out of harm's way. The first RPGs evolved out of wargames, and the goals were pretty straightforward: gain power and collect treasure. In order to gain fictional rewards characters had to take on risks, entering trap-filled dungeons and battling monsters. Under these conditions, minimizing risk to maximize rewards is just playing to the strength of the game.

Playing protectively is partially a self-defense mechanism. We've already covered how intimate the connection between players and their characters can be. If you're really connected to your character, the events of the game—in a sense—are happening to *you*. At the very least, they're probably happening to someone you care about. That kind of emotional bleed is totally natural. One way of dealing with it is keeping a PC out of situations that court danger.

This sort of approach is also enforced by the group. PCs address challenges together. When one player introduces risk, everyone has to deal with the results. Without a group enthusiastic about adding to the stakes, risky choices seem selfish. Staying in line with behavior that benefits the group makes collaboration easier.

This kind of storytelling *can* be really compelling. It's fun to watch someone think their way around big problems, using wit and skill to find solutions. There's an element of competition to this approach, not necessarily between the PCs and the GM, but between the characters and their circumstances. It relies on an almost antagonistic world constantly placing challenge between characters and rewards. There are plenty of players who really like this format for RPGs and plenty of games structured to support it.

WHY CHANGE THE FORMULA?
RPGs function perfectly fine as storytelling engines with PCs playing protectively. It's reasonable to question the need to change the classic formula. Playing protectively definitely works for some stories, but it doesn't work for all of them. It limits the range of what you can accomplish narratively.

If a character never makes a decision that creates challenge, then it is the GM's responsibility to create conflict proactively. This can come off as aggressive or malicious. If a party uses information only to avoid peril it can feel like withholding or obscuring information is the only way to create stakes. Trying to lure characters into vulnerable positions to make encounters exciting can easily feel unfair, especially because the GM has absolute control over the conditions of the world. Without strong communication, there is real danger of conflict brewing outside the game.

In noir, protagonists chase information into dangerous situations. A case can lead a detective to upset powerful people, take beatings, and get in gunfights. No reasonable person would want to do those things. Especially when the reward is answers to questions no one else is asking. Genres like horror, drama, and romantic comedy depend on characters being shortsighted or even self-destructive.

Protective play also closes characters off from vulnerability. This includes physical and emotional vulnerability. A PC trying to protect their character can instinctively downplay emotional situations that make them feel threatened or shy from investing in important relationships. That reduces the risk the character faces of being hurt, but it also lessens the opportunities for fun storytelling moments.

If the goal of an RPG is to win, in the way you might claim victory in a board game or video game, then playing protectively makes sense. If your goal is to create a compelling narrative, then opening yourself up to a range of options by knowing how to take risks will serve you better.

Looking for Trouble

In many ways, the philosophy of *looking for trouble* is a simple change in priority. You still want to see your character and party succeed; you just want that process to be a little more interesting. In looking for trouble the assumption is that choices that raise stakes create narrative momentum and open up possibilities. Rather than looking to protect a PC from danger, looking for trouble is trying to find actions that feel true to the character but probably make things worse.

In improv, performers are encouraged to *make interesting choices*. Improv scenes are a heightened version of the real world. Characters admit to feelings, stand up for beliefs, and grow as people. This is all stuff that *can* happen in real life but is rare. An interesting choice can veer away from expectation or lean into it. Ideally, interesting choices present scene partners with wide possibilities for creating a compelling transformation.

Doing what's safe or realistic runs counter to the philosophy behind making interesting choices. We don't want to see the ten thousand times tempers flare up and die out in traffic; we want to see the one time characters get out of their cars to shout. In a narrative-focused game, looking for trouble asks you to figure out what it takes to get your character to the point where they leave the car.

THE SPOOKY DOOR

Your character shouldn't feel forced into the kind of narratively convenient incompetence we sometimes see in movies. Horror especially is full of characters who continually make choices that put them in harm's way. If it feels like a character's circumstances are driven by easily avoidable mistakes, it makes it more difficult for the audience to identify with them. We still want to see the story move though—which brings us to the *spooky door*.

> *At the end of a long hallway, our protagonist confronts a door. It feels ancient, covered in carvings of skulls, demons, and indecipherable runes. Darkness seems to leak from it like a fog, but its most terrible features are lit just well enough....The handle seems to call out with a swell of eerie music.*

Spooky doors show up in various forms in many stories. They are obvious danger markers that also drive events. We know enough about storytelling to understand that this door is bad news. We also know as storytellers that it *has* to be opened. A player working defensively here will take pains to avoid opening it, because they're trying to be smart. Ultimately the door opening is inevitable. The story is structured to explore the action surrounding that event, so this choice merely delays the game.

A player looking for trouble will try to find a good reason for their character to open the door and explore the consequences. The challenge in the scene is no longer preventing a character from suffering harm, but justifying an action that feels ill-advised. Looking for trouble helps you treat this moment as an opportunity to make a statement about the character.

The GM bears some responsibility in giving their spooky doors reasons to be opened, but PCs have to come halfway. In its most critical form, looking for trouble is about generating narrative momentum. In its ideal form, looking for trouble provides PCs new opportunities to define their characters.

STRENGTH THROUGH WEAKNESS

Many games treat character weaknesses as a drawback, something a player would find undesirable. In certain contexts this is true; mechanical weaknesses usually limit your options, allowing you to accomplish less. Character flaws, however, open your possibilities to new and interesting opportunities.

Taking the idea of looking for trouble further, PCs can start to look at their character as a proactive catalyst for interesting events. Fictional heroes have flaws and motivations that allow them to dig deep into a problem before finding a way out.

Asking yourself simple questions can inspire actions that add new and interesting stakes to a scene:

- Is there something here that might tempt me to take a risk?
- What strongly held belief might blind me to something obvious to another person?
- What point of pride can I not afford to let go?
- Who am I trying to impress?
- What limitation do I refuse to acknowledge?
- What answers do I believe will set me free?
- Is there something I'm underestimating?

Answering these questions will help you find flaws tied to what defines a character. Any trait related to one of those questions can lead a PC to doing something impulsive, self-serving, or even foolish. The actions that follow will add complexity to the plot, giving the GM and other PCs the opportunity to escalate excitement.

WHAT SEEMS FUN?

Looking for trouble as a PC gives you agency over the kind of excitement you want to explore. When the GM creates scenarios, they are theoretically designed to appeal to you in some way. Taking action to court a specific kind of danger allows you to put yourself in circumstances you want to explore.

For example, it's a GM decision to create a high school where the faculty is a cult using students as sacrifices. As student PCs, you're definitely obligated to confront that situation. How you do it is up to you, which means you have a chance to define the form that threat takes.

Sneaking into the teacher's lounge to steal documents makes a scene where the danger is discovery and overt punishment. Testing out which teachers and administrators are involved in the cult creates a political tension where discovery provokes suspicion. Setting fire to the gym where the sacrifices take place provokes direct confrontation and outside attention.

All of those choices will create a certain atmosphere and lead to a specific danger. They put the PCs in the position of deciding how they want their story to unfold. Rather than making a choice based on what will strictly be safest for a party, looking for trouble can be about what kind of excitement you're most interested in seeing. The safety of a veiled political standoff between adults and teens is only worth it if it's more fun to you than an open chase scene in the halls.

Creating Agreement

As we've said before, being a PC means being a part of a team. RPGs are also built on collaboration. When looking for trouble, it's important to be mindful of how your choices impact the other players.

Online gaming forums have no shortage of stories about problem players who engage in frustrating behavior only to justify it by claiming, "It's what my character would do." The spirit of looking for trouble is finding fun in exploring character and heightening the plot. It's about creating cheers of excitement, not groans of frustration. If what you're doing when looking for trouble upsets your fellow players, it's not making the game more fun.

Looking for trouble challenges some of the basic assumptions about how RPGs are supposed to be played. Playing out the actions of a character working to steal something is actually different than telling an interesting story about a heist. These goals can coexist at a table, but the group needs to communicate to make that work. Let's look at some steps that will allow us to introduce this play style productively.

STEP 1: STATE A GOAL

Your group needs to understand what you want out of looking for trouble. If folks know what's going on, they'll even be able to actively support you. Without any conversation, looking for trouble can feel like a willful disregard for the circumstances of the game. Framing your thoughts as a concrete goal will help ensure that a move looking for trouble isn't just chasing chaos.

Omar is running a frontier sci-fi space punk game. His players are outlaws looking to pull a heist on a casino orbiting Mars. Lisa is playing Mohammed, a pickpocket with a high perception skill. He's been assigned a lookout position, but Lisa knows he's egotistical, and she thinks that might make his story role more interesting.

Omar (GM): *Let's check in with Mohammed. He's supposed to be keeping an eye on the security team.*

Lisa: *Yeah, I think he's actually one drink deep, hitting on the bartender in a conversation where they are both complaining about their bosses. He's not really paying attention.*

Omar (GM): *So he's not looking at all?*

Lisa: *Yup!*

Joe: *What? No, if he doesn't watch the guards we're going to get caught slipping into the vault.*

Lisa: *It's what he would do though!*

Without communication, this feels like a total slap in the face to the other players who are trying to make their plan work. They're all playing characters who are depending on Mohammed to do the job he was assigned. As a result, the choice to be a bad lookout feels like a lack of cooperation from Lisa as a player—not authentic characterization of Mohammed. Let's have Lisa state her goal to clear this up.

Omar (GM): *Let's check in with Mohammed. He's supposed to be keeping an eye on the security team.*

Lisa: *I think this scene might be more fun if Mohammed lets his pride get him into some trouble.*

Omar (GM): *What did you have in mind?*

Lisa: *He wanted a bigger role than being a lookout. What if he screws up a simple part of the lookout job because he was complaining—in vague terms, of course—to the bartender?*

Joe: *Couldn't he just do his job?*

Lisa: *He should, but I took a major flaw of prideful, so I don't think he's mature enough. I want to see that play a part in how this unfolds. I still want to do the mission; I just want Mo to do something that will get him chewed out later.*

Joe: *Ugh, come on, Mo...*

In establishing her goal, Lisa allowed her fellow players to understand what she really wants from her character deviating from the plan. It helped Joe understand that Lisa still wants to keep things on track; it's just going to look different because the character is flawed. Now she's collaborating instead of disrupting.

STEP 2: ESTABLISH BOUNDARIES

Part of making a session more fun for everyone is not totally hijacking the action. Lisa wants to have Mohammed's impulsive behavior make his job harder, but she also doesn't want to ruin the mission for everyone else. In order to do that, she's got to work with her GM to keep the scene in scope while exploring a personal story.

Omar (GM): *So what did you have in mind here? If Mo misses the guards they are going to catch the rest of the team.*

Lisa: *If he was doing his job right, he'd have time to work out a clever way to delay the guards. I want his options to be limited so he has to do something desperate. I'm comfortable with him suffering for this, but I don't want it to hit the group unless I fail a bunch of rolls.*

Omar (GM): *Okay, we'll avoid pulling other characters into this unless the dice really turn on you. But it's okay to make Mohammed take a few hits even if he succeeds?*

Lisa: *Yup!*

Omar (GM): *Everyone's okay with that?*

Joe: *I mean, as long as I still get a chance to crack this safe, I'm into it.*

Stating boundaries up front lets Omar know what kind of consequences the table is expecting. If Lisa's decision to role-play her flaw resulted in guaranteed setbacks for everyone in the group, it's easy for people to feel upset about the way things might go. Knowing the kind of consequences Lisa expects lets the group separate her decision from failures they would have experienced anyway. It also gives Omar the opportunity to play to Lisa's comfort level.

STEP 3: CHECK IN

Agreeing to one choice does not mean a group is ready to accept every possible choice that might follow. So far Omar's players are okay with the idea of Mohammed being forced to think on his feet and get hurt in the process. The consequences for that choice are only relevant to one character right now. Depending on Lisa's decisions the situation could escalate beyond what people agreed to. Keeping an open line of communication will help players stay within the group's comfort zone.

Omar (GM): *The bartender is pretty far into a long story about how she's constantly getting asked to work overtime when Mohammed gets a chance at a perception check.*

Lisa: *I rolled a 15.*

Omar (GM): *Yeah, the guards you need to keep an eye on are moving right past the bar.*

Lisa: *Okay, Mo is in panic mode. He's going to bolt at them without a plan.*

Omar (GM): *Is he attacking?*

Lisa: *No, more like suddenly running into them. Should I roll a deception?*

Omar (GM): *I think the guards will assume you're an idiot before they will assume you're trying to stop them. You smack into the pair and hit the ground with a thud. The guard you hit stumbles but doesn't go down. He looks furious. "What the hell is wrong with you, pipsqueak? Watch where you're going!" The bartender runs over and says "I think he was trying to ditch his bill!" What do you do?*

Lisa: *They called him pipsqueak? Mo's proud. He might actually take a swing at this guy; he has been drinking.*

Omar (GM): *You can, but I think outright attacking these guys is going to really escalate this. Even if you beat these guys, the rest of the casino staff is definitely going to arrest you. That will put the plan in real jeopardy.*

Lisa: *You're right; that's probably too far. I think he wants to, but something stops him.*

Joe: *It's Codex's voice saying "Mo...this is your conscience....You're going to get everyone killed."*

Lisa: *Yeah, something like that! He pauses and looks between the guards and the bartender. "I- I- thought I saw my boss, and he doesn't know I ditched work! You have to hide me!"*

Omar (GM): *Ha! Roll a deception and add plus-1 for working in your conversation earlier.*

Lisa: *With the plus-1 that's 9.*

Omar (GM): *One of the guards grins. "We can get you out if you settle your tab...and our tab; 50 credits or this gets loud."*

This check-in allowed Lisa the chance to consider how far she really wanted to take the complication she was adding to her lookout scene. Deciding not to start a fight kept her within the boundaries the group originally set. In the end, Lisa got a more dynamic story beat for Mohammed without hurting the overall heist. Although Joe was a very mission-focused player, he supported Lisa's fun because he knew it wasn't going to affect his. With communication a group with protective and troublemaking PCs was able to work together. Keeping communication in the open will allow your group to do the same.

Delegating Creativity

Our final advanced playing technique involves changing one of the central structures of traditional RPGs. In the introduction, we noted that GM responsibilities typically call for control of every aspect of the game world not influenced by the PCs. Most players assume that means the GM has to *personally* create all of those things. In reality, control just means the GM has final say. It's well within the spirit of the GM role to delegate certain creative tasks to other players. Session Zero is structured to give every player a hand in developing their game, which helps players connect to the fiction. There is no reason that kind of collaboration has to stop once players formally begin the game.

In this chapter, we'll take a closer look at the division between PC and GM and suggest techniques to improve your game by allowing other players to take on some of your responsibilities.

GM versus PC

Some folks think of GMs as not technically players because the role functions so differently than PCs. It's an understandable perspective. Most of what the PCs can do in the game world is defined by the rules. PCs can certainly attempt ideas that weren't anticipated by game designers and have no representation on character sheets, but it's up to the GM to make those ideas work.

The GM is allowed to dictate reality through a game's rules. In most cases, a GM won't decide how an alien parasite attacks a space commando, as that will be covered by mechanics. GMs *do* decide how many parasites are in a given location, how noticeable those parasites are, and how hostile they are toward space commandos. The ability of a PC to affect the fiction is limited by their creativity and the rules. The ability of a GM to affect the fiction is limited by their creativity and their judgment.

GMs also have authority over how to apply and interpret most rules. Some games even give them special information PCs don't have access to. If you look at the game as some kind of competition—the way some players do—these are clearly uneven positions. Even accepting that just participating in a game makes you a player, GMs are clearly not experiencing the game in the same way.

WHY DOES THE GM ROLE FUNCTION THIS WAY?

The idea of the GM as a sort of referee who is necessary for play but participates differently is actually inherited from the role's historical roots. RPGs developed from wargames where opposing players controlled competing armies. Some wargames were complex and required a neutral party or "marshal" to make judgments in circumstances where opposing players could not agree.

Older wargames mostly dealt specifically with combat and didn't provide guidance beyond what happened on the battlefield. The wargaming fandom developed these skirmish games into the foundation for military campaigns that had multiple players battling over resources or territory. This helped the rules-focused marshal role transform into a game master who crafted scenarios and dictated the outcome of events.

There's still a lot of practical function in the idea of a GM acting as rules martial. The scope of what can happen in an RPG is limited only by the power of imagination. Even a really well-designed game is going to run into situations where the proper application of the rules is not clear. Having one person with the authority to make a decision prevents arguments and allows the game to avoid pedantic pit traps.

Similarly, granting a player authority over the reality of the game world makes it easier to create agreement among players. People bring all kinds of good ideas to the table and sometimes you need someone to pick *one*. Having a GM also means PCs don't have to create their own challenges. This allows PCs to be surprised by their environment and react authentically to unforeseen events.

Ultimately, having a GM means someone at the table has the power to answer questions. That makes the structure of RPGs much easier than free-form creative writing.

Dave Arneson, the cocreator of *Dungeons & Dragons*, laid the groundwork for role-playing by crafting elaborate campaign scenarios that continually expanded the responsibility and creativity required by the game master. He eventually used *Chainmail*, a game designed by Gary Gygax and Jeff Perren to focus on single characters rather than large armies, to run his "Castle Blackmoor" campaign. This was the beginning of the play style that became RPGs!

WHY WOULD WE WANT TO CHANGE THAT?

Like any rule in an RPG, the GM role is flexible depending on the needs of the group. If a GM can decide when the group needs to worry about carrying capacity, they also get to decide if they need total authority over the NPCs, scenario, and setting. While the traditional GM structure has its merits, there are plenty of games that function excellently without GMs.

The big benefit of occasionally delegating GM powers to players is that it makes the game more personal. We already know people love seeing their ideas supported in the story; this just creates a new opportunity to do that. It gets rid of unnecessary guesswork too. You don't need to guess what might interest your party if you just *ask* them.

Allowing other players to portray NPCs can help manage chaotic scenes. Sometimes talking to the party means juggling the agenda of five separate NPCs who happen to be present. It's difficult for even really skilled GMs to split their attention that way. Dialogue between the PCs and a group of NPCs flows more naturally if there are more people able to represent the NPC group.

Delegating creative tasks doesn't completely do away with structure. It's always there when you need to return to it.

Collaborative Building

The easiest and most versatile kind of creative delegation is *collaborative building*. This is simply inviting non-GM players to contribute details and ideas to the world of the game. The scope of this collaboration varies from simple aesthetic choices to ideas with sweeping plot implications.

Though delegation is conceptually very simple—asking for contributions—it can be intimidating if you've never done it. To help you structure this kind of delegation we'll break down methods of soliciting ideas based on what you might be looking to open up.

ALWAYS STATE AN OBJECTIVE

In order to make meaningful and useful contributions players need to understand the purpose of what you're asking for. If you don't have an agenda it's fine to ask, "Can you each give me one detail about *X*?" However, if you want the PCs to help you create an intimidating death machine, you'll need to provide some guidance. That's usually as simple as framing your questions:

- This is a large city where you'll have the opportunity to sell cargo. What about this place lets you know you have come to the right place?
- What's something about this creature that makes your blood run cold?
- How can you tell you're facing a capable warrior?
- Among the piles of mundane treasure, you find something that makes your heart race with excitement. What is it?

You can also bluntly state your objective for your scenes before soliciting ideas. The goal is to have all the contributors working to support your agenda. Even with advanced techniques, your goal is clear communication.

FOCUS ON FEELING

What characters see, hear, and feel makes up the narrative and dictates the most important aspects of the audience experience. *Sensory* and *emotional* information are the keys to helping your players connect to the fiction. By asking the right questions you can help players generate their own experience based on what they want to see.

SENSES

Sensory details draw players in and ground them to a scene. When asking for sensory details you are trying to get players to connect to aspects of the fiction through sight, sound, smell, taste, and touch. Pick something you want a player to expand on and frame your question through one of the five senses.

SAMPLE QUESTIONS
- Why does this building look out of place?
- How does holding this weapon let you know it's the gun of an experienced killer?
- You smell something that reminds you of home. What is it?
- What about her voice reminds you of a person you trust?
- What kind of music do they play in this bar?

FEELINGS

Feelings help characters develop relationships with their environment as well as the people and things that populate it. Starting with the emotion you want characters to feel and asking players to describe what creates that feeling will help you guide the narrative in your desired direction while allowing PCs to stay true to themselves.

SAMPLE QUESTIONS

- What about the way these people are dressed sets you on edge?
- Hearing the sadness in his voice brings back a memory of loss. What is it?
- What here makes you smile?
- When the diplomat sees you, you catch a flash of emotion on their face. What was it?
- An item no larger than a tissue box sets your heart racing. What is it?

LOCATIONS

The environment is the catalyst for all sorts of exciting player choices, which means it's the perfect opportunity to solicit PC input. You can use details players choose to contribute to get a sense of what they're interested in doing there.

The larger the location your players are helping you create, the greater potential impact their ideas can have on the world. A detail in a single room can easily drive a scene. A detail about a city can pre-cipitate the action of countless scenes and influence the world of the game.

The consequences of details in small locations will typically be more immediate. A chandelier is something characters swing around on, a wall covered in bloody handprints is something to investigate, and a scruffy-looking detective is someone to talk to. All those actions are likely to resolve quickly. On a larger scale, a black market is a place to find and move goods; a museum is a place to find information or steal something valuable; a police station is a collection of potential allies, enemies, and informants. All of that potential won't be resolved in a single scene or even a single session.

SAMPLE QUESTIONS
- What here is interesting?
- What here is challenging?
- What here is useful?
- What here is mysterious?
- What here is dangerous?

WHAT'S GOING ON?

Asking about action occurring in locations lets players create opportunities and obstacles they're interested in exploring. This is a really easy way to create interesting plot hooks.

SAMPLE QUESTIONS
- Why is it difficult to find a room at an inn right now?
- It sounds like there are shouts coming from ahead. What are they saying?
- You see decorations in public spaces marking some kind of event. What do they look like?
- This place is known for a specific type of competition. What is it?
- Barriers have been placed around intersections for a kind of civic parade. Why do you find the procession strange?

PEOPLE

A GM can play dozens to hundreds of characters over the course of a campaign. It's natural that some end up better developed than others. Inviting players to share the burden gives you the opportunity to have a larger roster of engaging characters without adding extra work.

NPCs add personality to a scene. They give a direct voice to certain themes and help you shape the plot. Giving away control over something so big can feel really intimidating. However, involving other players can actually make some NPCs better equipped to fit their roles. Sometimes your baritone buddy just has better tools to make a memorable alien bouncer.

To set a player up for success in taking over an NPC all you need to do is give them easy-to-understand goals—just like the ones you had them create for their characters in Session Zero.

RUMORS

Asking your party for rumors about an NPC allows you to cast a net for useful character traits and history, without having to commit any of it to truth. Framing the question around an understanding you want your party to have about the character gets them where they need to be, and you can pick what fits best.

SAMPLE QUESTIONS
- What's a story you have heard about her strategic skill on the battlefield?
- What's something others swear he has done that you can't bring yourself to believe?
- Based on the rumors you have heard, what surprises you about the way this person looks?
- You once told a lie about this person to a stranger in a bar. What makes you think you might have been right?
- What's the most expensive object this emperor is supposed to own?

NPC ROLE-PLAY SHEET

✏ **Name:**

✏ **Concept:**

✏ **Goals:**

Small

Medium

Large

A frequent frustration for some GMs is introducing NPCs with a specific purpose, only to have the party fail to treat them in a way that allows them to fulfill their function. It takes a lot of power away from a final boss if no one takes them seriously. You can sidestep this problem entirely by having your PCs suggest character traits that will lead them in the right direction.

Simply asking, "What's something about this person that lets your character know they are a threat?" or "This person's reputation precedes them, what have you heard?" can save you the trouble of guessing how to engage the table. It's a simple matter of folding new ideas into what you already need the character to do.

REWARDS

Collaborating on objects is easy using the standard approach of asking for sensory or emotional details. Some objects in games serve a special role as narrative rewards. This could be treasure in a fantasy adventure, a medal in a military game, or a piece of evidence in a police procedural. Rewards work best when they create a relationship with the character and player who receive them. A treasure only matters if you treasure it.

Getting players to connect with a fictional object is much easier if they have a hand in its creation. Delegating details, or even handing over the power to completely design their own rewards, will help you create spoils that really make players feel victorious. Giving away this power also opens up big opportunities for you down the road. If a player is invested in something they own, you can use it to motivate them to action.

MAKE IT THEIRS

Getting players to invest personal details into the rewards they receive helps punctuate moments of victory. The very small gesture of personalizing a reward can have a big impact.

SAMPLE QUESTIONS
- The pile of treasure sparkles even in the low light. What attracts your attention first in all this splendor?
- The badge they slide across the desk is definitely yours. How can you tell they've given you a different gun?
- You can taste the minister's bitterness in the retraction they were forced to write. What sentence will provide you satisfaction for years to come?
- One item in the uniform that comes with your new rank feels deeply satisfying to hold. What is it and how does it look?
- This fight leaves you with a scar that really complements your features. What does it look like?

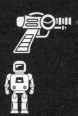

PART 3

Playing for Experience

The best way to learn narrative techniques is by playing. Even when you're armed with really good information, it takes practice to make use of it. This part of the book features a mix of exercises and tools to help solidify the lessons in Parts 1 and 2. Some of these exercises are meant to be practiced alone. Others work with a partner or small group. You can even integrate a few into your regular game sessions!

Finding a Voice

Silly voices are a proud RPG tradition. They add energy to a game and personality to characters. Many folks don't realize the range they have as voice actors until they dive in and try. Part of that is not knowing where to start. This exercise will help you generate and practice character voices.

Step 1: Genre and Archetype

Roll a d6 or pick a genre from the six in the table, then roll again for a character archetype. Your archetype doesn't have to be tied to the genre it's sorted under. You can mix and match! A wizard from a sci-fi or modern setting will sound different than one from a fantasy setting.

1 Fantasy	**2** Horror	**3** Sci-Fi
1 Wizard	**1** Witness to something terrible	**1** Robot
2 Mysterious hooded figure		**2** Hacker
	2 Librarian	**3** Humanoid alien
3 Tavern keeper	**3** Vampire	**4** Alien
4 Talking animal	**4** Killer	**5** Starship captain
5 Deity	**5** A human transformed into a beast	**6** Pilot
6 Dragon	**6** A creature too horrible to describe	

4 Modern	5 Historical	6 Apocalyptic
1 Politician	1 Peasant	1 Scavenger
2 Retail worker	2 Soldier	2 Raider
3 Police officer	3 Pirate	3 Bounty hunter
4 Student	4 Religious official	4 Mutant
5 Social media influencer	5 Noble	5 Cult leader
6 Activist	6 An actual historical person	6 Time traveler

Step 2: Attributes

Roll for or choose at least one attribute for your character from among the lists of possibilities in the table. These attributes will add greater distinction to the way your character sounds.

1 Age	2 Descriptor	3 Emotion
1 Child	1 Prim	1 Irritated
2 Teen	2 Slovenly	2 Glum
3 Adult	3 Flirty	3 Nervous
4 Middle-aged	4 Debonair	4 Cheerful
5 Elderly	5 Shy	5 Serious
6 Ageless	6 Tough	6 Disgusted
4 Era	**5 Quirks**	**6 Attitude**
1 Medieval	1 Played by a known celebrity	1 Condescending
2 1800s	2 Has an accent	2 Friendly
3 1940s	3 Speaks slowly	3 Overworked
4 1980s	4 Speaks quickly	4 Pretentious
5 1990s	5 Has a deeper voice	5 Desperate
6 Contemporary	6 Has a higher voice	6 Mature

Step 3: Practice

To practice speaking as your character, pick one of the activities listed.

ACTIVITIES

O Explain the plot to one of your favorite movies, novels, or video games.

O Describe your dream vacation and why you want to go to the place you chose.

O Pretend you are calling in sick to work and describe increasingly elaborate symptoms.

O Explain the water cycle or some other simple scientific fact.

O Talk about a dream you once had.

O Complain about your least favorite city or TV show.

Even changing a single attribute can alter your character's voice. Explore how a Condescending Teen Alien is different from a Nervous Teen Alien. Also, take note of how the words you choose change with your voice. Discoveries you make portraying big, wild characters will help you when doing more subtle character work.

Limiting Choices

As a PC a big part of your role is solving problems. It's easy to fall into patterns, using the same abilities to overcome every challenge that comes your way. It's definitely fun to play to your strengths, but if your solutions get repetitive the game can start to feel stale.

Imagine Solutions

To help you break patterns and keep your ideas feeling fresh, this exercise asks you to imagine solutions to problems without your usual tools. Each prompt poses a challenge you might encounter in an average gaming session. Following each prompt is a list of limitations you face that might change your usual approach.

 See how many limitations you can work your way around! In all situations assume you are acting alone.

GET PAST A GUARD
O You can't call attention to yourself.
O You are not allowed to use complex tools or magic.
O You can't use violence.
O You can't talk to anyone.

OBTAIN AN ITEM YOU CAN'T AFFORD

- ◯ You are not allowed to steal.
- ◯ You cannot lie.
- ◯ You cannot damage anything.
- ◯ The owner won't willingly part with the object.

LEARN A PIECE OF INFORMATION YOU DON'T KNOW

- ◯ No one is willing to tell you.
- ◯ You are not allowed to use complex tools or magic.
- ◯ No activity that takes you less than an hour will be effective.
- ◯ It's not written in a language you can understand.

GET TO THE OTHER SIDE OF A LARGE WALL

- ◯ You can't use any skill that relies on raw strength.
- ◯ You are not allowed to use complex tools or magic.
- ◯ You must do it within twenty-four hours.
- ◯ You must not destroy anything more solid than a sandcastle.

FIND A PLACE TO SLEEP

O You cannot spend money.

O You may not use any skills you use to fight opponents.

O You are far from any property that would make this simple.

O You cannot coerce anyone into a specific behavior.

ESCAPE CONFINEMENT

O You may not cause harm to another being.

O You don't have access to your most familiar tools.

O You must not draw too much attention to yourself.

O You cannot be completely unseen.

Same Rock, Different World

Genre and theme have a tremendous impact on how we construct a world. They can change what an object looks like and what we want people to see when they look at it. This exercise will challenge you to change common objects based on the style and themes of their setting.

Step 1: Pick a Genre

 Roll a d20 or choose a genre from the following list. You can even roll twice to create a hybrid genre or make up one that you feel is missing from the list.

1	Fantasy	**11**	Utopian
2	Sci-fi	**12**	Dystopian
3	Near future	**13**	Naturalistic
4	Far future	**14**	Punk (as in "cyber" or
5	Historical		"steam")
6	Horror	**15**	Adventure
7	Mystery	**16**	Mythic
8	Alien (extraterrestrial or	**17**	Modern
	simply unlike normal life)	**18**	Comedy
9	Apocalyptic	**19**	Tragedy
10	Slice of life	**20**	Animation inspired

Step 2: Identify Themes

Once you have your genre, decide what it means to you.

✐ **Identify three key themes you would focus on in a game within this genre. There can be more themes, but these three should be obvious and important you.**

These themes can be character- and story-driven such as "fear" or "good defeats evil." They can also be aesthetic such as "magic" or "natural beauty."

Step 3: Look at Objects

The following objects exist in a number of different settings in some form or another. Decide what you want players to think about when they look at objects like these. Then decide how that shapes the text you'll use to describe the object.

A KNIFE

Knives can be everyday tools or weapons. A knife can illicit all sorts of emotions depending on the circumstances under which characters encounter it.

What should the audience think about when they look at this?

What is the most common form of this object that would exist in this setting?

Where would a character encounter this?

Describe this object:

A PERSONAL VEHICLE

Technology and era have a dramatic impact on what personal transportation looks like. The economic circumstances of a setting determine who has access, which also shapes appearance.

✎ **What should the audience think about when they look at this?**

✎ **What is the most common form of this object that would exist in this setting?**

✎ **Where would a character encounter this?**

✎ **Describe this object:**

A BOOK

They hold all kinds of knowledge both mundane and forbidden, which means books can represent all sorts of themes.

✎ **What should the audience think about when they look at this?**

✎ **What is the most common form of this object that would exist in this setting?**

✎ **Where would a character encounter this?**

✎ **Describe this object:**

A COMMUNICATION DEVICE

We tend to think of communication as a modern innovation, but people have been sending messages for thousands of years in a myriad of ways. Communication can happen through letters, horns, flags, and smoke. How people communicate says a lot about your world.

✏ What should the audience think about when they look at this?

✏ What is the most common form of this object that would exist in this setting?

✏ Where would a character encounter this?

✏ Describe this object:

A LIGHT

Lights are a part of everyday life, and that means when they change it's a big statement. Lights also have a big impact on mood, which is closely tied to theme.

✎ **What should the audience think about when they look at this?**

✎ **What is the most common form of this object that would exist in this setting?**

✎ **Where would a character encounter this?**

✎ **Describe this object:**

Building the Group Mind

A strong improv ensemble needs the ability to quickly pursue the same goal and make room for every member to contribute. Part of that is cultivating comfort and familiarity with one another's ideas. While each performer brings a unique perspective to the group, it helps if everyone is thinking along similar lines. Improvisers refer to the skill that enables this collaboration as "the group mind."

"The group mind" sounds like something PCs might battle in an RPG, but it's actually a useful thing to cultivate. A party with a strong group mind collaborates more effectively and has similar priorities. The three exercises in this chapter are extremely easy to do at a gaming table and will help players develop collaborative skills.

Zip-Zap-Zop

This is one of the most simple and widely taught improv exercises. It calls for participants to stand or sit in a circle facing one another. A single participant starts the game by pointing at another and saying "Zip!" That player will point to another and say "Zap!" The third player will point to yet another player and say "Zop!" At which point the sequence will start over with "Zip," and the sequence repeats until the group decides to move on.

The game starts slowly but should develop a progressively faster pace. A group loses Zip-Zap-Zop if one of the words is said out of the correct order: a "Zip!" following a "Zap!" for example.

GOALS

In Zip-Zap-Zop players try to keep the sequence flowing as quickly as possible while maintaining a simple pattern. Players need to be ready to receive the sequence and pass it off reflexively. It's even more valuable if players try to avoid falling into patterns—such as always pointing to the same player—and work to ensure the group is passing the sequence with an even distribution.

HOW IS THIS HELPFUL?

This simple game cultivates focus. Players need to be ready and watching in order to receive and pass on the sequence without breaking the rhythm. Once the game reaches a certain pace it's really noticeable when someone hesitates or misses a cue. To go really fast in Zip-Zap-Zop players need to be focused on each other. That is a really good habit to have at a gaming table.

Adding the layer of avoiding patterns helps players consciously avoid falling into predictable habits. That mentality will encourage players to bring new ideas to each session. Evenly distributing the sequence cultivates an atmosphere of care. It's easy to get caught up in the events of a game and not notice when someone is falling behind. Having the ability to engage in a high-pressure situation while minding who *isn't* involved is extremely useful.

Finally, Zip-Zap-Zop is *silly*. Prioritizing and pursuing extremely frivolous goals is part of what defines the RPG experience. Caring about Zip-Zap-Zop is a good first step to caring about all sorts of silly things.

CHALLENGE YOURSELF

If you want to make Zip-Zap-Zop more challenging, remove pointing from the game. Players will have to pass the sequence just by using eye contact. That requires much more focus!

Count to Twenty

Counting to twenty is one of the more difficult introductory improv exercises, but it seems deceptively simple. A group must count to twenty with one person speaking at a time. No one person can say two numbers in a row. If you say "one" you need to wait until someone else says "two" before you say "three." Otherwise, any player is allowed to say a number at any time. During the game, players may not say anything that isn't a number. If two people speak at the same time you lose and the group must start over from "one." You also lose if the group reaches twenty and not everyone has participated.

GOALS

This game has a fairly straightforward goal of reaching twenty. The challenge is reading the group to avoid stepping on each other's toes. If everyone waits for someone else to speak, the group will never make progress. If everyone jumps in to say the next number, the group will constantly have to start over.

Players will have to learn to communicate nonverbally to signal when they are about to say a number. Once a group is comfortable with the format, they should also avoid using hand signals and learn to communicate exclusively through eye contact and facial expressions.

HOW IS THIS HELPFUL?

Like Zip-Zap-Zop this game is about cultivating focus on the group. Players really need to pay attention to one another in order to succeed. This is a game about contributing and making space. After playing for a while, players learn how to find their moment and then let someone else take the stage. This is extremely valuable in an environment where everyone is enthusiastic about making a contribution.

To really make this exercise challenging, ask players to close their eyes while they play. This changes the focus of the exercise from nonverbal communication to exclusively developing a rhythm as a group. It seems impossible at first, but groups with a well-developed group mind can make it to twenty fairly regularly.

You can also try to get to twenty within a certain time limit. The added pressure makes everything more challenging.

Jinx

This exercise is challenging but also more creatively fulfilling than the others. Players should stand in a circle or sit at a table where everyone can see each other. Two players start the game by facing one another and saying the first word that pops into their minds on the count of three. In most cases, this will produce two different random words. Once everyone in the group knows which words were said, play will continue clockwise with one of the original players turning to the person on their other side. On the count of three they will say the word they believe is conceptually halfway between the random words that were just said.

The goal is to get a pair of players to say the exact same word at the same time. Although only two players are active at a time, everyone else in the group should think of their own answer as they count down.

EXAMPLE

Liz and Tyler face each other on the first round of Jinx.

Group: *3... 2... 1...*

Liz: *Death!* **Tyler:** *House!*

Liz turns to Johnny and they think of their next word as the group counts down.

Group: *3... 2... 1...*

Liz: *Mausoleum!* **Johnny:** *Tombstone!*

Johnny turns to JPC.

Group: *3... 2... 1...*

Johnny: *Pyramid!* **JPC:** *Pyramid!*

GOALS

Finding the halfway point between two concepts is an interesting creative challenge, but the real objective is to get players to start thinking like each other. The only way to win is if the players learn to quickly consider their thoughts along with the thoughts of their friends.

In the early stages, thinking of a halfway point between two unrelated words is a big distraction. People's minds work remarkably differently, and it's difficult for thoughts to align without effort. Learning how to anticipate what word someone thinks is halfway between two concepts is a step toward understanding how they think.

At first groups struggle to produce even a single jinx. With time, a seasoned group can create them within a few rounds.

HOW IS THIS HELPFUL?

This is the purest form of a warm-up, as it calls for your group to practice listening and collaborating in a micro format. The skills you need to succeed at Jinx are the closest to the skills you need to collaborate while playing an actual game. You don't need to be "good" at Jinx to be successful in your role-playing; it's just a really good way to jump-start your collaboration skills.

Unpacking Desire

RPGs offer pretty diverse experiences. Sometimes a bad experience with an RPG says more about the way you feel about the specific game than about role-playing itself. This exercise will help you understand yourself better as a player so you can seek out the games that will let you have *your* kind of fun.

I DON'T KNOW YET!

New players, or folks who have played for a while but never asked themselves these sorts of questions, might not know how to rate these statements. That's okay! Now that you're looking for them you can come back later and fill this out with more confidence. It's also possible your tastes will change as you become comfortable with RPGs or develop as a person.

The statements in this exercise are by no means a comprehensive inventory of how you can engage with a game. As you play you will stumble upon statements that more accurately describe you, and you can develop them based on this exercise.

Step 1: I Like...

To start we're going to identify what you feel is most important.

 Look at the statements below and rate them from 1 to 5, 5 being most accurate for you and 1 being least accurate:

I like to speak in character: _____

I like to see a lot of action: _____

I like to get in fights: _____

I like to feel the emotions my character is feeling: _____

I like to feel like I have beaten my enemies: _____

I like to feel challenged by overcoming obstacles: _____

I like to win without feeling like I'm in real danger: _____

I'm more interested in character's relationships than abilities: _____

I get satisfaction out of world building: _____

I like using familiar, simple tools to solve problems: _____

I love animals and I want to deal with them in games: _____

I like robots because they are big and destructive: _____

I like big machines because they are complex and delicate: _____

I want to be swept away by romance: _____

I want to watch two characters grow closer: _____

Once you're done, take a look at the statements you rated at 5, or at least the ones you rated the highest.

✎ **Choose three of them and ask yourself how they relate to each other:**

If you gave 5 to "I like to win without feeling like I'm in real danger" and "I like robots because they are big and destructive," the power fantasy in many RPGs is a driving force for your enjoyment. Right away we can intuit you'll have more fun in games that help you feel like a badass. If you selected "I like to feel like I have beaten my enemies" and "I like to feel challenged by overcoming obstacles," you might get more satisfaction from tactical- and strategy-based experiences. Selecting "I like to feel the emotions my character is feeling" and "I like to get in fights" means you might be more compelled by the emotional journey of someone who makes decisions in risky situations regardless of the outcome.

The ability to identify what you like about games will empower you to seek more fulfilling experiences. It can help you make big decisions, like which game system you'll enjoy or which genre holds the most appeal. It will also help you make smaller decisions that might come up during play. Is it really better to go with the safe, diplomatic solution if you almost always have more fun when a fight breaks out? It could be if you're the sort of player who draws enjoyment from entering combat only when you hold the advantage.

Step 2: Examine Your Experience

Once you examine the relationship between your biggest "likes," answer the following questions so you can apply that understanding to how you approach games:

📝 **Is there a part of the game where my likes show up more frequently?**

📝 **Is there a genre that really supports what I like?**

📝 **Is there a role in the game that I want to play that gives me tools to engage with what I like?**

📝 **Do I have the freedom to create my own space for what I like when it is not present in the game?**

📝 **Does the game provide tools to shorten aspects of play that I don't enjoy as much?**

📝 **Can other players fill roles that I don't find compelling?**

Answering those questions will help you structure your game experience around the aspects of play you find most enjoyable. Finding the right game system or character options will help you set yourself up for success.

Step 3: Making Your Own Space

Finally, after checking in with your core motivators, and using those to structure your big pregame decisions, you need to be mindful of what small moments during play factor into your larger desires.

To do that, think about moments that support your favorite aspects of play. We'll identify those as goals for each gaming session. Instead of hoping for the right moments to appear, you can chase after them yourself. You can also ask your fellow players to help you find the specific fun you're looking for.

List several behavioral aspects of play ("goals") that will facilitate the kind of gameplay you like:

A good goal should be a small component of a larger idea that you have fun with. If you enjoy getting in fights, break it down into a manageable aspect of that like "drawing first," "doing a lot of damage," or "taking down an enemy."

ASSIST ROLL

To help you make your own goals here's a list based on the author's tastes:

- Make a joke in character. (I like to speak in character.)
- Speak with emotion in my voice. (I like to feel the emotions my character is feeling.)
- Explain something new about the world. (I get satisfaction out of world building.)
- See characters kiss. (I want to be swept away by romance.)
- Be a part of a meaningful conversation. (I want to watch two characters grow closer.)

Narrative Rewards Table

Plenty of games have tables to roll on to reward PCs with material treasures. If your group is more interested in the story, then they'll be more excited to see plot hooks than gold.

 Roll a d100 or two d10s to generate a random narrative reward to give a PC.

1–5	The impression that they have been betrayed
6–10	Knowledge of a critical error with little time to correct it
11–15	An opportunity for revenge
16–20	The return of someone from their past
21–25	A secret they can share with only a few
26–30	A responsibility of extreme emotional importance
31–35	An appreciation for something they once despised
36–40	A connection with someone they think of as an enemy

41–50	An opportunity to gain something valuable that they can pay for later
51–55	A favor from an influential NPC
56–60	A brief moment of intimacy
61–65	Respect from an opponent
66–70	Approval from a mentor
71–75	Forgiveness for a past misdeed
76–80	A mistake turned out to actually benefit them in the long term
81–85	The satisfaction of knowing they were right
86–90	A lasting connection with someone important
91–95	The courage to express a masked emotion
96–99	A new sense of purpose
100	Peace with a problem they have long grappled with

Pacing Scorecard

There is a lot of information to keep track of when pacing a game. It's easy to lose sight of who is getting what out of each session. This tool will help you plan for a session by helping you track changes in scale and type, the general tension level of your story, and which players are served by each scene.

The Grid

This 5×5 grid represents an individual session for a game. Each column represents a scene. Most three- to four-hour gaming sessions have three to five scenes depending on the type of scenes involved.

High threat,
story
climax

**Tension
Level**

No threats,
receiving
rewards

	1	2	3	4	5

Scenes

Plenty of groups play shorter sessions, while other groups play for longer. Don't worry if you end up having less than three or more than five scenes. This is an average approach, not an ideal to strive for.

The rows represent the general level of unresolved tension in a narrative. If the game is just starting or the PCs have just wrapped up a storyline, a scene is probably on one of the lower rows. If the party is facing a boss, the scene will be on a higher row.

In a game following the adventures of a crew of pirates a scene chart might look like this:

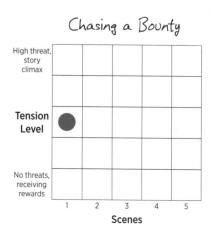

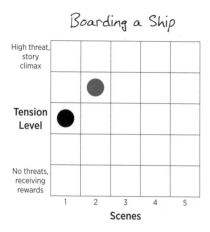

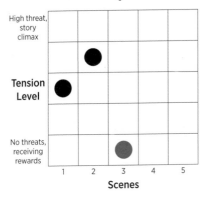

Distributing Treasure

(chart) Tension Level — vertical axis: "High threat, story climax" (top) to "No threats, receiving rewards" (bottom). Horizontal axis: Scenes, 1 2 3 4 5.

MOVING SCENES ON THE GRID

Both upbeats and downbeats can move tension in either direction. Generally speaking, action and challenge scenes will resolve tension; discovery and preparation scenes will build tension; and interpersonal and emotional scenes will process tension. There are no hard rules for what moves a scene up or down on the grid; it's best to evaluate based on the expected outcome of your scene.

Under normal circumstances, events in a scene will start the following scene one row higher or lower on the grid. This represents the natural movement of the plot in a long-form story. It's possible to have adjacent scenes maintain the same level of tension, but ideally, you want to avoid this. Too many scenes in a row where tension doesn't build or release makes a game feel stagnant. Even if you're maintaining a consistently high level of tension, it runs the risk of exhausting players.

It's also possible to have a scene cause tension to rise or fall more than one row. This is usually the result of a plot twist that dramatically raises the stakes or a climax that resolves major plot threads. That kind of extraordinary story event is fun every once in a while, but too many will make a game feel scattered and give the audience whiplash.

You can't plan for everything. Your party can and will surprise you. This chart won't lock in your plans, but it will help you evaluate how to react when things don't go the way you expected.

SCENE CARD

🖊 **Scene Number:** _____

🖊 **Type (circle all that apply):** action, discovery, interpersonal, emotional, challenge, preparation

🖊 **Players (check one box for participation, two for spotlight, and three for heavy focus):**

⭕ ⭕ ⭕ _____

⭕ ⭕ ⭕ _____

⭕ ⭕ ⭕ _____

⭕ ⭕ ⭕ _____

⭕ ⭕ ⭕ _____

⭕ ⭕ ⭕ _____

🖊 **Scene Title or Events Summary:**

_____

_____

_____

_____

_____

_____

_____

_____

_____

The scene number will tell you where this scene belongs on your scene grid. Your scene types will help you track changes in type. The PC section will help you track which PCs are featured in a given scene and how they are featured. Finally a title or summary will help you track your general idea for what is supposed to happen.

CHANGE IN TYPE

For the same reasons you want to move the tension level from scene to scene, you should try to avoid repeating the same scene type too many times in a row. Even a group that loves to role-play will get fatigued if every scene has an interpersonal focus.

As you lay out scene cards on your grid, take note of which scene types you're incorporating and how they are positioned. Try to avoid gathering the same scene type three times in a row. Even if the way you incorporate a particular scene type changes, there is a danger of overloading one kind of experience. For example, a chase followed by a fight and an escape seems exciting narratively. They're all action scenes though. They also tend to resolve and relieve tension. It's also likely that you'll spend part of these scenes in initiative, which means they're going to play long.

NOT EXACTLY A RULE OF THREES

The advice on pacing here just provides general guidelines. It's possible to group similar scene types together if you pay careful attention to making them feel distinct. Be advised that doing so is a challenge.

It's great to have all of that action in one session, but it will have a greater impact if you break it up. You might place an interpersonal standoff scene between the chase and the fight, or add a short preparation scene between the fight and the escape. That will create a greater balance and provide the audience with a chance to build and process tension.

PLAYER SCORE

Having so many PCs to track for audience experience can feel overwhelming. Using the scene card you can give yourself a rough idea of how each player is being served. The higher a PC's score, the more engaged they are as part of the audience.

1 Box	2 Boxes	3 Boxes	
Participation	Spotlight	Heavy Focus	Bonus Points
The player is engaged, but not the central focus: Participating in a group scene. Getting a player spotlight in a scene where their PC is not present.	This means getting to be an important part of a given scene: A PC competence spotlight. Participating actively in a character scene. A plot point important to the PC is addressed in the scene. Advancing a character goal.	The scene is heavily focused on the experience of a single PC to the point it feels made for them: Participating in a character scene. The scene is built around the PC's personal narrative. Accomplishing a character.	+1: A session is dedicated to a character's goals or backstory. +1: A personal antagonist is menacing the group.

Check boxes on your scene card according to the most significant aspect of a scene for the player. For example, a combat-focused character in a group combat would check two boxes because their competency spotlight makes their role in the group scene more significant.

Ideally in a session with five scenes you'll want a player to have around 8–10 points. You'll notice that smaller scenes by default grant more points. Smaller playgroups naturally have an easier time engaging each player. That also means point averages in small games should be a little higher.

BALANCING ACT

It's okay if a session favors one or two PCs over the rest of the group. However, it's important to be aware of when that happens. Two sessions in a row focusing on the same characters cuts out part of your audience. It's a good idea to communicate with your group when you anticipate an unbalanced session to confirm they are onboard to support the idea of certain characters taking center stage.

Mood Lighting

Tone is part of how we communicate with our fellow players. Part of the goal in storytelling is communicating tone through narrative. Saying "This place is full of shadows and skulls" is more fun than stating "This place is dangerous." To help you understand how tone can change an environment we're going to look at a specific place and change how we describe it based on a shifting tone.

Step 1: Choose a Genre

As we saw in Chapter 17, genre is important for deciding how something looks. It's much easier to create when you have something to build on, and genre provides a strong foundation.

 Roll a d6 or choose a genre you're comfortable working with:
1. Fantasy
2. Sci-Fi
3. Horror
4. Dystopian
5. Historical
6. Modern

If you're looking for an added challenge, roll more than once to combine two genres!

Step 2: Build a Room

Now it's time to make your canvas. Imagine a room that can comfortably fit around eight people.

🖉 **Answer some basic questions:**

How is this room lit?

How do people get in and out?

Is there much furniture?

Has this place been decorated?

🖉 **Identify three distinct features of the room:**

These will be focal points for you—features that you will reference as the room changes. They should be distinct enough to help people understand your genre but flexible enough to carry different themes. A crystal orb is good because it signals the genre and has some flexibility. A human skull is less useful because it's harder to fit into nonthreatening contexts.

📝 **General description of your room:**

Step 3: Set the Scene

Now it's time to see how this place changes based on the tonal needs of your scene. All of the details you created in Step 2 will be present in the scenes you are about to set. Details like lighting, order, position, and presentations *can* change. The words you use to describe certain objects and the details you focus on should also change.

Each of the following scene prompts has three theme prompts included with it. Your goal is to use the details in your room to communicate the themes in each prompt.

CONFLICT

Someone is about to fight. The stakes will be high and the rewards will be important. Fights are often physical in RPGs, but they can also be emotional arguments. Your goal is to make this room a tool to heighten your conflict and explore the excitement. Themes: danger, survival, strife.

📝 **What ambient features like lighting, sound, and temperature have changed the most?**

✐ What new detail would allow this room to better fit its new context?

✐ Introduce this room to a group seeing it for the first time in this context:

✐ Which feature will be most useful to characters in the scene to come?

✐ Describe that feature in a way you feel would entice a character to interact with it:

✐ Which feature will best allow two characters to interact?

✐ Describe the details of that feature that would make that interaction possible:

REST

This is a safe place in between moments of action. There is no danger here, and the party will have an opportunity to unwind and recover. Your goal is to let your group know they are free to use this place as they wish. Themes: safety, comfort, peace.

What ambient features like lighting, sound, and temperature have changed the most?

What new detail would allow this room to better fit its new context?

Introduce this room to a group seeing it for the first time in this context:

Which feature will be most useful to characters in the scene to come?

✎ Describe that feature in a way you feel would entice a character to interact with it:

✎ Which feature will best allow two characters to interact?

✎ Describe the details of that feature that would make that interaction possible:

REVELATION

This room will provide important answers. It wants to draw players in and cause them to ask questions. Your goal is to help your group understand that there is significant information here if they are willing to look. Themes: mystery, knowledge, investigation.

✎ What ambient features like lighting, sound, and temperature have changed the most?

✎ What new detail would allow this room to better fit its new context?

✐ Introduce this room to a group seeing it for the first time in this context:

✐ Which feature will be most useful to characters in the scene to come?

✐ Describe that feature in a way you feel would entice a character to interact with it:

✐ Which feature will best allow two characters to interact?

✐ Describe the details of that feature that would make that interaction possible:

Side Scenes

Sometimes the main game isn't enough; you want a different context to explore your character, or to just get some privacy in your story-telling with some personal play. Side scenes that happen around or outside the continuity of your main game are a great way to develop your character. Thankfully improvisers and fan fiction authors have been developing formats for this kind of storytelling for years, and they make great minigames.

This chapter will give you three side scene exercises you can use to spend more time with your favorite character.

Forty Minutes after a Disaster

This game is a character relationship study that puts two characters in a situation where they are forced to have conversations they normally wouldn't. This side scene starts just after some kind of mishap has trapped them in a confined space. Help is on the way, but they know they will not be freed for at least a few hours. Enough time has passed that it is no longer relevant for either character to mention their predicament in conversation, but there is nothing to do but talk to one another.

Begin this exercise by filling in this statement:

"**We are** ....
character name 1

and ....
character name 2

We are ....
best summary of their relationship: "friends," "rivals," etc.

We are currently ....
summary of their predicament

and there is nothing left to say about it."

Then choose one of the following moves:

REVEAL AN INTEREST

One character will start a conversation based on something they are passionate about. This is something that should be inconsequential or barely explored in their day-to-day life as a hero.

 Roll a d6:

1-**2**: This interest uncovers a fundamental disagreement between characters.

3-**4**: This interest explores an aspect of the world.

5-**6**: This interest creates unexpected common ground between the two characters.

EXPRESS A CURIOSITY

A conversation starts based on information one of the characters doesn't know. This is something they have wondered about silently and never really had the opportunity to discuss before.

 Roll a d6:

1-**3**: The curiosity is about the outside world, and no one has an answer. The characters speculate together, each revealing something about the way they see the world.

4-**6**: The curiosity relates to one or both of the characters in the scene. Someone has an answer, and the pair ask each other questions until the truth is uncovered.

UNCOVER A SECRET
One or both of the characters discover something they had not previously understood. Even if one or both of the characters had suspicions surrounding this secret, the conversation it sparks is totally new.

☀ **Choose Two:**
- O The secret is based on unresolved emotion.
- O The secret has never been shared before.
- O The secret is somehow dangerous.
- O The secret involves someone both characters know well.
- O The secret is related to one of the character's past.
- O The secret is related to the relationship between both characters.

The characters talk until they resolve that the secret should no longer be hidden, or they vow to share its burden together.

BETWEEN MOVES
After each move time passes.

☀ **Choose one of the following vignettes to describe before making a new move:**
- O Both characters manage to make their space more comfortable in a small way.
- O Each character finds a moment of fleeting privacy.
- O The appearance of one or both characters changes noticeably.
- O There is a moment of needed physical contact.

ENDING THE SCENE

When both characters are finally rescued, they share a brief moment of eye contact.

✏️ **With this look, both characters communicate the following sentiments:**

You can trust that I will never speak about:

From now on I will treat you differently by:

Although we endured this together, this will never change:

Five Times and One

A classic fan fiction format is "Five times they didn't and one time they did." It explores five short scenes of a character failing to do something and one scene in which they manage to pull it off. This series of prompts will guide you through creating a story in this format for one of your PCs.

STEP 1: FIGURE OUT WHAT THE CHARACTER IS TRYING TO DO

✴️ **Choose Two:**
- ○ It's something small and personal.
- ○ It's emotionally significant.
- ○ It will bring them great joy.
- ○ They dread it fiercely.
- ○ It will fundamentally change their life.
- ○ It involves another person.

SUM IT UP IN A SENTENCE:

"This is a story of five times (*character name*) didn't (*the action you're exploring*) and the one time they did."

STEP 2: CREATE YOUR SCENES

Each prompt below has a reason the character failed to perform the action you chose.

Figure out how each obstacle stopped them and write it down in a scene or bullet points.

They ran out of time.

They were stopped by another person.

A sudden event made it impossible.

They didn't notice how close they were to doing it.

They stopped themselves.

Why was this time different? Why was that enough?

Coffee Shop AU

Sometimes to really get to know a character, stuff them into a setting that isn't theirs. Fan fiction authors do this by creating an alternate universe (AU) where their favorite characters encounter slice-of-life challenges—for instance, running a business. This game can be played alone or with a group. Everyone is acting as both a GM and a PC. Just follow the steps below to make discoveries in your own AU.

STEP 1: CREATE THE WORLD

- **Choose a business:**
  - O Coffee shop
  - O Flower shop
  - O Barbershop/salon
  - O Hotel
  - O Record store
  - O Tattoo parlor
  - O Bar

- **Assign roles:**
  - O Manager
  - O Senior employee
  - O Junior employee
  - O Temp/intern
  - O Regular customer
  - O Bookkeeper
  - O Delivery person
  - O Landlord

- **Choose two styles:**
  - O Classic
  - O Rockabilly
  - O Trendy
  - O Punk
  - O Goth
  - O Upscale
  - O Family
  - O Futuristic
  - O Choose your own

- **Pick one asset:**
  - O Great location
  - O Popular
  - O Beloved
  - O Cool

- **Pick one problem:**
  - O Financially insecure
  - O Falling apart at the seams
  - O Technically illegal
  - O Protested by the community

- **Your antagonists are (choose two):**
  - O A rival business
  - O Greedy investors
  - O Ornery customers
  - O Unsympathetic authorities
  - O Your own incompetence
  - O Bad luck

STEP 2: PICK A SCENARIO
Now it's time to figure out what's going on!

SOMEONE...
- O Customers
- O Employees
- O The community
- O Your rivals
- O Well-meaning parents
- O Fate itself

CAUSED...
- O A street festival
- O A surprise inspection
- O A talent show
- O An unexpected delivery
- O A celebrity guest appearance
- O A natural disaster

AND...
- O Half of the staff is gone
- O Something important broke
- O Rent is due tomorrow
- O There are snakes!?
- O You can't accept credit cards
- O Someone's crush is here

WHICH MEANS...
- O You have one chance to get this right
- O Someone could get fired
- O You'll have to be in two places at once
- O You might have to close permanently
- O There is too much business for you to handle
- O Your dreams might come true

STEP 3: PLAY IT OUT

Based on your scenario, decide what your characters are doing.

✎ **Every time you encounter a situation where the outcome of a character's actions is unclear, roll d6 to find out what happens. Gain a die if:**

○ You're acting in the best interest of the business.
○ You're doing something that matches your style.
○ Everyone is working together.

Based on your highest roll consult the following chart to see what happens next:

ROLL CHART
1 A cartoonish misfortune makes everything worse.
2 They get what they want but fail to notice a major complication.
3 They have to make a compromise to succeed.
4 Someone butts in where they are not supposed to.
5 Things go almost suspiciously better than expected.
6 You witness an actual miracle.

The side scene ends when you close for the day.

Glossary

actual play (AP)
A form of entertainment that involves recording, streaming, or otherwise exporting a session of an RPG as a kind of performance. Performers in actual play productions are still playing the way any group would, though their decisions may account for the presence of an external audience. Actual play is also sometimes called *live play* or *real play*.

audience
Anyone engaging with the story of a game. For most groups, that means the players at the table, both PCs and GMs. RPGs are distinct from most other storytelling mediums because the audience is also actively participating in drafting the fiction. The audience can also include nonparticipating observers, which is the case with many actual play productions.

check
In many RPGs a check is a game mechanic that calls for a character to determine their success using a randomizer. For instance, an athletics check might call for a player to roll a die or draw a card to determine their character's ability to perform a physical feat. The specific word used to describe a check varies based on game system, though *check* is a popular term.

downbeat
A moment or scene in a story that allows the audience to build or process tension. Downbeats support high-intensity upbeats and help make a story engaging. Downbeats are rarely the most exciting parts of a narrative, but they make exciting moments possible.

experience (XP)

Experience is a mechanical system many RPGs use for advancing characters. PCs are awarded a number of experience points or "XP" after various encounters and challenges in the game. These points represent the knowledge and skills they acquired on their journey, allowing them to become stronger. In some systems accumulated XP automatically advances a character's level, in others the points are spent like currency on specific new abilities.

fiction

Broadly, fiction is information regarding imaginary events and characters. In RPGs the fiction is the content of your game. It refers to any information in your shared imaginary space. When we use "fiction" in this book it refers to the explicit shared reality between the players.

game master

A special player type that shows up in many RPGs. Game masters, or "GMs," guide the narrative, have agency over the game world, and portray non-player characters. They have a more organizational role than the other players and are often said to "run" RPGs.

immersion

Immersion is experiencing a deep connection to the events of a game. It can take many forms. Some players experience immersion through emotional bleed or when they get swept up in storytelling. Others experience immersion when they feel the mechanics of a game are properly simulating fictional events. Yet more derive a sense of immersion through props, costumes, and other atmospheric elements. Immersion is not an essential experience for satisfying gameplay or narrative, but it can enhance the experience for some players.

initiative

Initiative is a common term for a method of portraying chaotic action clearly and resolving competitive situations fairly. Initiative calls for players to decide a clear order of action, usually determined by a randomizer. It's essentially an elaborate methodology for taking turns. Time is usually protracted in initiative; a few seconds of action might take hours of narration to play out.

medium

The materials used to create a work of art and the format through which a piece of art is enjoyed. Books, films, TV, and podcasts are all different mediums for storytelling.

module

A prepared scenario for an RPG. Modules have information about characters, locations, and situations accompanied by game information.

non-player character (NPC)

Non-player characters, or "NPCs," are supporting characters in the story of an RPG. They can be allies and antagonists with varying levels of importance, but their general purpose is to make the journey more interesting for the PCs by providing resources, challenges, and, opportunities for role-play. They are usually—but not always—portrayed by the GM.

objective

Your objective is what you and your group want out of a game. It can be a broad idea like "I want to have fun" or "I want to tell a good story." It can also be extremely specific to your experience like "I want to talk like a pirate" or "I want my character to punch the mayor." Keeping objectives is a way of outlining your hopes for a game so you can actively pursue the kind of experience that will make you happy.

personal play

An aspect of the RPG experience that a player enjoys alone or outside of traditional gaming sessions. This encompasses activities like building characters, crafting adventures, creating backstory, making props and accessories, maintaining notes, or even just thinking about your game.

Lots of games depend on personal play activities, but few formally recognize it as part of the game. For some players personal play activities are the most enjoyable aspect of RPGs. It's a rich and underexplored part of the hobby.

player

Anyone actively participating in a game. This includes both GMs and PCs. In some spaces people use *player* exclusively to refer to the PC role. We do not follow that convention in this book.

player character

The main characters in an RPG story. Players in the "PC" role are usually focused on portraying a single character. This portrayal is based around making decisions about a character's actions and motivations and embodying them in voice.

randomizer

A tool used to add uncertainty to a game. This puts some aspects of the game out of control of the players. The most common examples are dice and cards, but games use all sorts of tools, including candles, coins, and wooden tumbling towers.

run or running (game)

A semi-colloquial term for the organizational work a GM does to facilitate a game narrative. Prompting PC action, portraying the game world, portraying NPCs, setting and ending scenes, and deciding which rules apply to which situation all fall under the umbrella of "running" the game.

session

An instance of a group playing a game. Game sessions can range from one to ten hours depending on the game and the group playing. Typically a session is composed of several scenes that move the narrative forward.

Session Zero

A meta discussion between players to establish goals for their games and common knowledge about their characters and setting. This discussion usually takes place at the start of a session or campaign before role-play begins. Session Zero discussions help avoid mismatched expectations and give players a foundation of knowledge, which helps them make stronger creative choices.

stats

The numerical or otherwise abstract values that represent story information in a game. For instance, if the game expresses a character's strength as a numerical value, that number is the character's strength *stat*. *Statting* something for a game is the act of breaking down story information into abstract values that work with game mechanics.

story beats

Significant events or scenes that define a character's journey through a narrative. "Upbeats" are high-energy scenes that resolve tension. "Downbeats" are lower-energy scenes that build tension.

system (game, role-playing)

A *role-playing system* is a set of rules that determines how a given game structures role-play. Different RPGs can have the same core *game system*. For example, the Powered by the Apocalypse system is used in games like *Apocalypse World*, *Bluebeard's Bride*, and *Monsterhearts*. When we refer to a game or role-playing system in this book we're mostly concerned with how rules shape the experience of play and narrative.

table

Both the physical table you play your game around and the players who play with you.

text

The specific words and actions that shape the understanding of the events of your game.

tone

The style in which a narrative is explored. A dark tone might include challenging themes and images, while a light tone cultivates a more accessible environment. Stories possess artistic value regardless of tone. A light story can be deep and meaningful; a dark story can be shallow and uninspired. In RPGs tone determines the kind of content your story focuses on.

traditional

Games modeled after *Dungeons & Dragons*. These games place emphasis on a stark difference between GM and PC roles, numerically based game information, and liberal use of randomizers.

upbeat (narrative)

An upbeat scene resolves tension through action. During an upbeat, tension reaches peak levels before resolving events and lowering the overall tension level of a story.

Acknowledgments

Thanks and acknowledgment to Avery Alder, Vincent and Meguey Baker, Epidiah Ravachol, John Harper, Alex Roberts, and Grant Howitt, who pioneered some of the storytelling mechanics that appear in this book. Your work continues to be an inspiration.

Additional Resources

Boss, Emily C. "Terms." *Black and Green Games*, 2007, www.black greengames.com/terms.

Campbell, Joseph. *The Hero with a Thousand Faces*. New World Library, 2008. (Originally published 1949.)

Peterson, Jon. *Playing at the World: A History of Simulating Wars, People and Fantastic Adventures from Chess to Role-Playing Games.* Unreason Press, 2012.

Portnow, James. "Differences in Scale vs. Differences in Kind: Keeping Players Interested." Extra Credits, 2013, https://youtu.be/TlBR1z-ue-l.

Index

Action scenes. *See also* Scenes
creating, 220–26
discovery for, 89–92
examples of, 143–46
imagery for, 142–46
initiative for, 43, 90, 129, 217, 237
rest between, 224–25
revelations for, 225–26
sensory details for, 137–46, 177
settings for, 127–31, 178–79,
220–26
story beats for, 116–17
violence and, 47–48, 127–31
Actual play (AP)
creating, 26–27, 58–59
definition of, 235
explanation of, 13–14
personal play and, 105–6
Advanced techniques. *See also*
Storytelling techniques
choices for, 109–19
conflict and, 162–72
delegating creativity, 173–83
explanations of, 107–83
for game masters, 109–19
imagery for, 135–48
personal style for, 109–19
for player characters, 149–65
themes for, 120–48, 193–99
traditional approaches and,
162–75, 240
The Adventure Zone, 14
Agreement, creating, 83–86,
167–72
Alternate universe (AU), 232–34
Apocalypse World, 239
Archetypes, 26, 187–88
Arneson, Dave, 175

Artistic expression, 101, 108–9,
121–22
Atmosphere, 66–68, 167
Audience
definition of, 19, 235
engagement of, 19–27, 87–99,
218–19
experiences of, 19–27, 87–99
explanation of, 19–27
pacing for, 87–99
perspective of, 20, 26, 63–65
separating from characters, 26
storytelling techniques for,
19–27

Backgrounds, 33, 66, 100, 130,
150–51
Backstory, 26, 37–44, 97–98, 106,
218, 238
Basic techniques, 14, 17–106. *See
also* Storytelling techniques
Bleed, 101, 163
Bluebeard's Bride, 239
Books, as objects, 197
Boss, Emily Care, 49, 101
Boundaries, establishing, 34, 49,
52, 71, 170–72
Bowman, Sarah Lynne, 49
Brown, Maury, 49

Campbell, Joseph, 149, 150
Cards, 215–18, 238
Chainmail, 175
Challenge scenes, 89, 92–95, 116,
125–26, 152–56, 214–16. *See also*
Scenes

Character goals, 33–34, 74, 180–82, 210, 218
Character levels, 88
Character optimization, 37–38
Character personality, 15, 26, 42–51, 94–96, 106, 180–82, 187–88
Character traits, 37–38, 52–57, 83, 97, 149–65, 180–82, 188–89
Character voices, 102–3, 142, 187–89
Character vulnerability, 100–106, 156–61. *See* also Player characters
Check
    athletics check, 235
    definition of, 235
    knowledge check, 136–37
    perception check, 171–72
    stealth check, 42
    strength check, 77–79
Choices
    advanced techniques and, 109–19
    agreement and, 83–86, 167–72
    collaboration and, 69–86
    honoring, 117–19
    importance of, 69–86, 109–19
    with intention, 109–19
    limiting, 190–92
    making, 69–86, 109–19, 164–65
    storytelling techniques and, 69–86, 109–19, 190–92
    of themes, 122–28, 138–39
The Chronicles of Narnia, 46
Cinderella adaptation, 20
Classic hero, 149–52. *See also* Heroes
Coffee shop AU, 232–34
Collaboration
    agreement and, 83–86, 167–72
    aiding, 28–35
    building, 176–78

connecting method for, 76–82
elaborating method for, 76–82
with group, 28–35, 45–68
improv and, 200–204
investing method for, 76–82
making choices and, 69–86
Session Zero for, 45–57
on settings, 50–51
storytelling techniques and, 28–35, 45–86
tips for, 58–68
Collective spotlight, 93–94. *See also* Spotlight
Comedy, 49–50, 124
Comic books, 46, 58–59, 104, 108, 151–52
Communication device, 198
Competence spotlight, 94–96, 218. *See also* Spotlight
Conflict, creating, 62–63, 162–72, 222–23
Count-to-twenty exercise, 202–3
Creations, story-led, 36, 39–44, 113–19
Creations, system-led, 36–44, 113–19
Creativity, delegating, 173–83
Critical Role, 14
Crossed Stars, 28–30

Desire, unpacking, 205–10
Dice, rolling, 12–13, 29, 37–39, 59, 67, 111–19, 238
Disagreements, handling, 70, 83–86, 167–72
Discovery
    expressing, 72, 89–92, 121, 167, 214
    for tension, 89–92, 167, 214
    for themes, 121
Discovery scenes, 89–92, 121, 167, 214, 216. *See also* Scenes

Downbeat scenes. *See also* Story beats
  definition of, 235, 239
  explanation of, 88–93
  for moving tension, 214–15
  storytelling techniques for, 116–17, 214–15
Drama, 49–50
Driving forces
  enthusiasm, 100–105
  explanation of, 100–106
  vulnerability, 100–106, 151–61
Dungeons & Dragons, 13, 175, 240
Dynamic play, 152

Emotional bleed, 101, 163
Emotional details, 101, 177, 182
Emotional exploration, 50, 66, 91–92
Emotional scenes, 89, 91–92, 214–16. *See also* Scenes
Emotions
  bleed and, 101, 163
  details for, 101, 177, 182
  engagement and, 100–106
  experiencing, 89–92, 100–106
  exploring, 50, 66, 91–92
  focus on, 177–78
  investment in, 101
  scenes with, 89, 91–92, 214–16
  tension and, 214–16
The Empire Strikes Back, 123
Engagement
  approaches to, 102–6
  of audience, 19–27, 87–99, 218–19
  basics of, 100–102
  bleed and, 101, 163
  description of, 100–102
  driving forces of, 100–106
  emotions and, 100–106
  enthusiasm for, 100–105

  lorekeeping and, 104–5
  min-maxing, 102
  personal play and, 105–6
  storytelling techniques for, 100–106
  voice and, 102–3
  vulnerability for, 100–106, 156–61
Enthusiasm, 100–105
Expectations, mismatched, 24–25, 28, 50, 239
Expectations, setting, 92–94, 130, 153
Experience (XP)
  actual play and, 105–6
  analyzing, 208–10
  of audience, 19–27, 87–99
  definition of, 27, 236
  emotions and, 89–92, 100–106
  experience points and, 27, 149–50, 236
  gaining, 185–234
  lorekeeping and, 104–5
  overall experience, 23–24, 27
Experience points (EPs), 27, 149–50, 236
Experiential competence, 94–95
Explicit reality, 60–63, 66, 72

Fan art, 104–5
Fan fiction, 104–5, 227–34
Fandom, 104–5, 174
Fiction. *See also* Storytelling techniques
  creating, 14, 17–106
  definition of, 236
  ensemble fiction, 131, 150
  fan fiction, 104–5, 227–34
  genres and, 31–33
  narrative and, 36–44, 58–68
Films, favorite, 19–23, 46, 66, 92, 104–8, 151, 189

Focus
    choosing, 139–41
    connections for, 140–48
    cultivating, 201–3
    on emotions, 177–78
    explanation of, 64–65
    giving, 98–99
    imagery and, 139–48
    importance of, 64–65, 98–99
    perspective and, 64–65
    sharing, 154–55
    taking, 98–99
    themes and, 140–48
Foreshadow technique, 130, 131

Game designers, 29, 49, 101, 106, 115, 173
Game masters (GMs)
    advanced techniques for, 109–19
    basic techniques for, 14, 17–106
    complaints about, 22–26
    creativity of, 173–83
    definition of, 14–15, 236
    delegating creativity, 173–83
    explanation of, 14–16
    generating rewards, 211–12
    improvisational style of, 109–19
    mechanics-driven GMs, 113–19
    personal style of, 15–16, 109–19
    playing for experience, 185–234
    power imbalance and, 16
    preparation skills of, 109–12
    railroading and, 22, 26
    role of, 15–16, 22–27, 109–83, 236, 238
    scorecard for, 213–19
    social dynamics and, 16
    spoiler trap for, 33–35
    story-driven GMs, 113–19
    story-led creations for, 41–42
    style of, 15–16, 109–19
    system-led creations for, 38–39

Game mechanics, 36–44, 113–19, 122
Game of Thrones, 46
Game sessions. *See also* Games
    definition of, 239
    explanation of, 13–16
    planning, 213–19
    power gaming, 37–38
    practicing, 186–90
    running, 15–16, 109–83, 236, 238
    Session Zero, 45–57, 173, 180, 239
Game systems. *See also* Games
    definition of, 15–16, 239
    role-playing systems, 13, 23, 36–44, 91, 113–19, 239
    selecting, 45–46
    system-led creations, 36–44, 113–19
    types of, 28–29
Games. *See also* Role-playing games
    choosing, 28–30
    comedy in, 49–50, 124
    connecting method for, 76–82
    drama in, 49–50
    elaborating method for, 76–82
    favorite games, 46–47, 62–63
    gender in, 48–49, 129
    improv for, 69–86, 104–6, 200–204, 227–34
    investing method for, 76–82
    length of, 46
    levels of, 46, 100–103
    min-maxing, 102
    mysteries for, 41, 51–52, 56, 90–91, 225
    objectives for, 28–35, 40–60, 160–69, 176–82, 200–210, 237
    power levels for, 46
    premise of, 30–31, 46

romance in, 29–30, 48–49, 66, 124–25
rumors for, 52, 180
running, 15–16, 109–83, 236, 238
safety tips for, 49
scenarios for, 30–39, 45–46, 78–85, 115–19, 233–34
scorecard for, 213–19
settings for, 45–51, 112–19, 125–31, 178–79, 193–99, 220–26, 231–34
sexuality in, 48–49
stats for, 36–44, 110, 133, 239
story-led creations, 36, 39–44, 113–19
system-led creations, 36–44, 113–19
traditional approaches to, 25–27, 106, 162–72, 238, 240
violence in, 47–48, 126–31
Gender, 48–49, 129
Genre
    archetype and, 187–88
    choosing, 31–33, 47, 187, 193, 220
    combining, 32–33, 193
    establishing, 45–50
    fiction and, 31–33
    patches, 132, 134
    shifting, 193–99
    themes and, 124, 132–34, 193–95
    types of, 28–33, 45–50, 124–26, 132–34, 163–64, 187–99, 207–8, 220
Gloomsprinter, 28–30
Glossary, 235–40
Goals. *See also* Objectives
    character goals, 33–34, 74, 180–82, 210, 218
    creating, 28–35, 210, 218
    establishing, 13, 33–34
    long-term goals, 46, 74

pursuing, 40–60, 154, 160–69, 176–82, 200–210
scenes and, 126, 153
stating, 28–35, 53–55, 168–69, 176–77
themes and, 126
Greene, Harrison, 49
Grid example, 213–19
Group
    collaboration with, 28–35, 45–68
    improv for, 200–204
    playing for experience, 185–234
    understanding narrative, 58–68
    working with, 28–35, 45–68
Group mind, building, 200–204
Gygax, Gary, 175

Hamlet, 20
Heroes, 33, 60–61, 83–86, 97–98, 149–52, 157–61
Hit points, 20, 42, 88, 135–36
Hooks, 45, 80–85, 97, 179, 211–12

Iconic hero, 151–52, 157–61. *See also* Heroes
Imagery
    advanced techniques for, 135–48
    chart for, 148
    connections for, 140–48
    creating, 126, 130, 138–48
    description of, 135–38
    examples of, 143–46
    focus and, 139–48
    for scenes, 141–48
    sensory details, 137–46
    themes and, 135–48
    uses of, 126, 130, 135–48
Immersion, 92, 100–102, 112, 236
Implicit reality, 62–63, 66, 72

Improv
  collaboration and, 200–204
  exercises for, 200–204
  explanation of, 69–86, 200–204
  fan fiction and, 104–5, 227–34
  for groups, 200–204
  lessons in, 69, 72–73
  side scenes and, 105–6, 227–34
  "yes and" philosophy, 69–75
Initiative
  action scenes and, 43, 90, 129,
    217, 237
  definition of, 237
  explanation of, 90, 237
  initiative-based action, 43
Interpersonal scenes, 89, 91, 214–
  17. See also Scenes

Jinx exercise, 203–4

Knives, 85, 195

Lighting, 59, 66, 127, 199, 220–26
Limitations, resolving, 190–92
Lines and Veils, 49
Listening skills, 72–75, 83–86, 110,
  204
Living narrative, 112–19. See also
  Narrative
Living world, 112–19. See also
  Settings
The Lord of the Rings, 46
Lorekeeping, 104–5

Mechanical competence, 94–95
Mechanical failure, 97
Mechanical support, 91–93, 134
Mediums
  definition of, 237

storytelling mediums, 19–23,
  54–59, 235, 237
types of, 19–23, 28–29, 54–59,
  92, 181, 237
Min-maxing, 102
Modules, 38–39, 237
Monomyth, 149–51
Monsterhearts, 239
Mood lighting, 59, 66, 127, 220–26
Movies, favorite, 19–23, 46, 66, 92,
  104–8, 151, 189
Much Ado about Nothing, 123–25
Music, 59, 66, 100, 108–9, 112
Mysteries, 41, 51–52, 56, 90–91, 225

Narrative. See also Storytelling
  techniques
  creating, 36–44, 113–19
  explanation of, 58–68
  fiction and, 36–44, 58–68
  living narrative, 112–19
  rewards for, 211–12
  story beats for, 87–95, 116–17,
    153, 172, 214–15, 235, 239,
    240
  tone of, 28–31, 46–50, 103, 118,
    126–32, 135–39, 220, 240
Non-player characters (NPCs). See
  also Player characters
  cast of, 51
  definition of, 15, 237
  explanation of, 15–16
  goals of, 180–82
  interpersonal scenes with, 89,
    91
  personality of, 15, 26, 42–51, 95,
    106, 180–82
  portraying, 161, 175–76, 236, 237
  role-play sheet for, 181
  rumors about, 180
  vulnerability of, 100–106,
    156–61

Objectives. *See also* Goals
   choosing, 43–44
   creating, 160
   definition of, 237
   expressing, 43–44
   pursuing, 40–60, 154, 160–69,
      176–82, 200–210
   stating, 28–35, 53–55, 168–69,
      176–77, 237
   storytelling techniques for,
      28–35
Objects, changing, 193–99
Objects, in games, 85, 132, 160, 177,
   193–99
Obstacles, 83–85, 90, 151–61,
   190–92, 206–7, 231. *See also*
   Problems
The OK Check-In, 49
One Shot, 14

Pacing
   basics of, 87–93
   character levels and, 88
   explanation of, 87–93
   hit points and, 88
   importance of, 87–88
   scale changes for, 87–88
   scenes for, 87–99
   scorecard for, 213–19
   spotlight factors for, 87, 89–91,
      93–98
   strategies for, 87–99
   tension and, 89–92
   type changes for, 87–88
Patches, 132, 134
Perren, Jeff, 175
Personal play, 105–6, 227–34, 238
Personal style, 15–16, 109–19
Personal themes, 131–34. *See also*
   Themes
Personality, 15, 26, 42–51, 94–96,
   106, 180–82, 187–88

Perspective, 20, 26, 63–65, 73,
   121–24, 130–32
Player characters (PCs). *See also*
   Non-player characters
   advanced techniques for,
      149–65
   archetypes, 26, 187–88
   backstory of, 26, 37–44, 97–98,
      106, 218, 238
   cast of, 28, 51–57, 131–32, 149–56
   complaints about, 22–26
   creating, 52–57
   definition of, 14–15, 238
   explanation of, 14–16
   favorite characters as, 41,
      227–32
   goals of, 33–34, 74, 180–82, 210,
      218
   heroes, 33, 60–61, 83–86,
      97–98, 149–52, 157–61
   interpersonal scenes with, 89,
      91, 214–17
   introducing, 52–57
   keeping together, 94
   levels of, 88
   min-maxing, 102
   naming, 59–61, 181, 215–16,
      227–28
   number of, 179–80
   optimization of, 37–38
   personality of, 15, 26, 42–51,
      94–96, 106, 180–82, 187–88
   portraying, 58–68, 93–103, 149–
      52, 161, 175–76, 236, 237
   practice for, 185–234
   as protagonists, 14–15, 24–33,
      89–97, 125–26, 131–32, 149–65
   relationships between, 55–57,
      153, 227–30
   role of, 14–15, 22–27, 173–83,
      190–92
   rumors about, 52, 180
   scorecard for, 213–19

Player characters
(PCs)—*continued*
separating from audience, 26
side scenes for, 227–34
social dynamics and, 16
spoiler trap for, 33–35
in spotlight, 87, 89–91, 93–98,
218
story-led creations for, 36,
39–44, 113–19
supporting cast of, 131–32,
149–50
system-led creations for, 36–44,
113–19
themes for, 120–48, 193–99
traditional approaches to,
162–75, 240
traits for, 37–38, 52–57, 83, 97,
149–65, 180–82, 188–89
transformation of, 153
voices for, 102–3, 142, 187–89
vulnerability of, 100–106, 156–61
Players. *See also* Player characters
advanced playing techniques,
107–83
as audience, 19–27
basics for, 13–15, 17–106
complaints about, 22–26
definition of, 238
explanation of, 14–16
playing protectively, 162–64
power imbalance among, 16
practice for, 185–234
questions for, 205–10
self-analysis by, 205–10
social dynamics and, 16
statements by, 205–10
Playing for experience
building group mind, 200–204
changing settings, 193–99
improv and, 200–204
limiting choices, 190–92
narrative rewards, 211–12

pacing scorecard, 213–19
practice and, 185–234
scorecard for, 213–19
shifting genre, 193–99
unpacking desire, 205–10
Playing protectively, 162–64
Plot hooks, 45, 80–85, 97, 179, 211–12
Plot spotlight, 97–98. *See also*
Spotlight
Plot themes, 120–48, 193–99
Posture, 62, 103
Power gaming, 37–38
Power imbalance, 16
Power levels, 46
Premise, 30–31, 46. *See also*
Scenarios
Preparation scenes, 89, 92–93,
214–17. *See also* Scenes
Preparation skills, 109–12
Problems, solving, 13–14, 23–28,
85, 132–34, 151–67, 190–92. *See
also* Obstacles
Protagonists, 14–15, 24–33, 89–97,
125–26, 131–32, 149–65. *See also*
Player characters

Quests, 211–12

Railroading, 22, 26
Randomizers, 13, 38, 59, 67, 119,
238. *See also* Dice
Reflection technique, 39–40,
130–31
Relationships, 55–57, 153, 227–30
Revelations, 225–26
Rewards, 182–83, 211–12
Role-play spotlight, 96–97. *See
also* Spotlight
Role-playing games (RPGs). *See
also* Narrative; Storytelling
techniques

advanced techniques for, 107–83
audiences for, 19–27, 87–99
basics of, 13–15, 17–106
benefits from, 13–14
choices for, 69–86, 109–19,
    164–65
collaboration on, 28–35, 45–86,
    200–204
comedy in, 49–50, 124
concepts for, 69–86
connecting method for, 76–82
definition of, 13–14
delegating creativity for, 173–83
differences regarding, 19–22
drama in, 49–50
driving forces for, 100–106,
    151–61
elaborating method for, 76–82
enthusiasm for, 100–105
explanation of, 12–16
gender in, 48–49, 129
improv for, 69–86, 200–204
investing method for, 76–82
length of, 46
levels of, 46, 100–103
min-maxing, 102
mood lighting for, 59, 66, 127,
    220–26
mysteries for, 41, 51–52, 56,
    90–91, 225
objectives for, 28–35, 40–60,
    160–69, 176–82, 200–210
pacing for, 87–99, 213–19
personal style for, 15–16, 109–19
power levels for, 46
practicing, 185–234
rewards for, 182–83, 211–12
romance in, 29–30, 48–49, 66,
    124–25
rumors for, 52, 180
safety tips for, 49
scenarios for, 30–39, 45–46,
    78–85, 115–19, 233–34

settings for, 45–51, 112–19, 125–
    31, 178–79, 193–99, 220–26,
    231–34
sexuality in, 48–49
stats for, 36–44, 110, 133, 239
story-led creations, 36, 39–44,
    113–19
system-led creations, 36–44,
    113–19
terms for, 13–16, 235–40
themes for, 120–48, 193–99
traditional approaches to,
    25–27, 106, 162–75, 238, 240
violence in, 47–48, 126–31
vulnerability for, 100–106,
    156–61
Role-playing systems, 13, 23,
    36–44, 91, 113–19, 239. See also
    Game systems
Romance, 29–30, 48–49, 66, 124–25
Rooms, building, 220–26. See also
    Settings
Rule systems, 13
Rumors, 52, 180

Safety tips, 49
Scale, changes in, 87–88. See also
    Pacing
Scenarios, 30–39, 45–46, 78–85,
    115–19, 233–34. See also Genre
Scene cards, 215–18, 238
Scene grid, 213–19
Scenes
    action scenes, 43, 47–48,
        89–92, 116–17, 127–31, 217, 237
    cards for, 215–18, 238
    challenge scenes, 89, 92–95,
        116, 125–26, 152–56, 214–16
    creating, 45–46, 125–31, 178–79,
        220–26, 231–34
    discovery scenes, 89–92, 121,
        167, 214, 216

Scenes—*continued*
  downbeat scenes, 88–93, 116–17, 214–15, 235, 239
  emotional scenes, 89, 91–92, 214–16
  goals for, 126, 153
  grid for, 213–19
  imagery for, 141–46
  interpersonal scenes, 89, 91, 214–17
  for pacing, 87–99
  personal play and, 105–6, 227–34
  preparation scenes, 89, 92–93, 214–17
  settings for, 45–51, 112–19, 125–31, 178–79, 193–99, 220–26, 231–34
  side scenes, 105–6, 227–34
  story beats for, 87–94, 153, 172, 239, 240
  theme and, 125–31
  types of, 89–99
  upbeat scenes, 88–95, 214–15, 235, 239, 240
Schrödinger, Erwin, 115–16
Schrödinger's Cat, 115
Schrödinger's Goblins, 115–18
Scorecard, keeping, 213–19
Script Change, 49
Self-analysis, 205–10
Self-awareness, 48
Self-knowledge, 22–24
Sensory details, 137–47, 177, 182
Session Zero. *See also* Game sessions
  characters in, 180
  for collaboration, 45–57
  definition of, 239
  design of, 173
  preparing for, 45–46
  storytelling techniques for, 45–57

Settings
  for action scenes, 127–31, 178–79, 220–26
  changing, 193–99
  collaboration on, 50–51
  creating, 45–51, 112–19, 125–31, 178–79, 193–99, 220–26, 231–34
  details for, 178–79
  examples of, 126–31
  objects in, 85, 132, 160, 177, 193–99
  theme and, 125–31
Sexuality, 48–49
Shakespeare, William, 20, 123–25
Shakespeare 2, 125
Sheldon, Brie Beau, 49
Short scenes, 230–31. *See also* Side scenes
Side scenes. *See also* Scenes
  coffee shop AU, 232–34
  exercises for, 227–34
  five short scenes, 230–31
  improv and, 105–6, 227–34
  relationship scenes, 227–30
Social dynamics, 16
Spoilers, avoiding, 33–35
Spotlight, 87, 89–91, 93–98, 218
Stats
  definition of, 239
  establishing, 36–44, 110
  thematic stats, 133
  types of, 36–44, 239
Stavropoulos, John, 49
Stokes, Tayler, 49
Stories, favorite, 21–22, 92, 110, 151, 189
Story beats
  for changing characters, 153
  definition of, 239
  downbeats, 88–93, 116–17, 214–15, 235, 239
  for pacing, 87–94

upbeats, 88–95, 214–15, 235, 239, 240

Story hooks, 45, 80–85, 97, 179, 211–12

Story-led creations, 36, 39–44, 113–19

Storytelling techniques. *See also* Fiction; Narrative
advanced techniques, 107–83
atmosphere, 66–68, 167
backstory, 26, 37–44, 97–98, 106, 218, 238
basic techniques, 14, 17–106
choices and, 69–86, 109–19, 190–92
collaboration and, 28–35, 45–86
conflict, 62–63, 162–72, 222–23
for engagement, 100–106
explicit reality and, 60–63, 66, 72
genre, 28–33, 45–50, 124–26, 132–34, 163–64, 187–99, 207–8, 220
hooks, 45, 80–85, 97, 179, 211–12
imagery, 126, 130, 135–48
implicit reality and, 62–63, 66, 72
improv and, 69–86, 104–6, 200–204, 227–34
mediums for, 19–23, 28–29, 54–59, 92, 181, 235, 237
music and, 59, 66, 100, 108–9, 112
pacing, 87–99, 213–19
perspective, 20, 26, 63–65, 73, 121–24, 130–32
practicing, 185–234
setting, 45–51, 112–19, 125–31, 178–79, 193–99, 220–26, 231–34
side stories, 105–6, 227–34
story beats, 87–95, 116–17, 153, 172, 214–15, 235, 239, 240

story-led creations, 36, 39–44, 113–19
system-led creations, 36–44, 113–19
tension, 26, 29, 89–92, 167, 213–17
theme, 120–48, 193–99
tone, 28–31, 46–50, 103, 118, 126–32, 135–39, 220, 240
traditional approaches, 25–27, 106, 162–75, 238, 240

Superheroes, 33, 60–61, 83–86, 97–98, 151–52

The Support Flower, 49

System-led creations, 36–44, 113–19

Systems, role-playing, 13, 23, 36–44, 91, 113–19, 239. *See also* Game systems

Table
defining, 240
encounter table, 114–21
engaging, 100–106
game table, 14–16, 22–28, 45–50, 62–65, 200–201, 240
rewards table, 211–12

Television shows, 46, 104, 189

Tension
building, 89–92, 214–17
creating, 26, 29, 89–92
discovery for, 89–92, 167, 214
downbeats for, 214–15
emotions and, 214–16
moving, 213–17
pacing and, 89–92
releasing, 90–91, 213–17
upbeats for, 214–15

Terms, defining, 13–16, 235–40

Text. *See also* Storytelling techniques
atmosphere and, 66–68, 167

Text—*continued*
  for collaboration, 58–68
  definition of, 240
  explicit reality and, 60–63, 66, 72
  implicit reality and, 62–63, 66, 72
  interpretation of, 59–62
  presentation of, 58–68
Themes
  advanced techniques and, 120–48, 193–99
  approaches to, 122–34
  choosing, 122–28, 138–39
  discovery for, 121
  explanation of, 120–21
  focus and, 140–48
  foreshadowing, 130, 131
  genre and, 124, 132–34, 193–95
  goals and, 126
  identifying, 194–95
  imagery and, 135–48
  patches, 132, 134
  personal themes, 131–34
  plot themes, 120–48, 193–99
  reflecting, 39–40, 130–31
  settings and, 125–31
  shifting, 193–99
  stats for, 133
  storytelling and, 120–48, 193–99
  underscoring, 66, 130, 147
Tone
  definition of, 30, 240
  establishing, 46–50
  lighting and, 59, 66, 127, 220–26
  of narrative, 28–31, 46–50, 103, 118, 126–32, 135–39, 220, 240
  shifting, 220
  varying, 103, 220
Traditional game approaches, 25–27, 106, 162–75, 238, 240

Traits, 37–38, 52–57, 83, 97, 149–65, 180–82, 188–89
Transportation, 32, 132, 196

Underscore technique, 66, 130, 147
Upbeat scenes. *See also* Story beats
  definition of, 235, 239, 240
  explanation of, 88–95
  for moving tension, 214–15
  storytelling techniques for, 214–15

Vehicles, 132, 196
Violence, 47–48, 126–31
Voice
  character voices, 102–3, 142, 187–89
  engagement and, 102–3
  finding, 187–89
  practicing, 189–90, 210
Vulnerability, 100–106, 156–61

Weapons, 85, 160, 177, 195
Words, utilizing, 58–68, 72. *See also* Text
Worlds, creating, 112–19, 125–31, 193–99, 231–34. *See also* Settings

The X-Card, 49

Zip-Zap-Zop exercise, 200–202

About the Author

James D'Amato is the creator and game master of the *One Shot* podcast, as well as several spinoff podcasts dedicated to RPG gameplay. He trained at Second City and iO in Chicago in the art of improvisational comedy. He now uses that education to introduce new people to role-playing and incorporates improvisational storytelling techniques to create compelling and entertaining stories for RPG campaigns and one-shot adventures.